LESSONS OF THE CONSTITUTION

Lessons of the Constitution

Student Workbook

for

*Promises of the Constitution:
Yesterday, Today, Tomorrow*

Pamela Romney Openshaw

Provo, Utah 2015

Works by the author:
Promises of the Constitution: Yesterday, Today, Tomorrow
Lessons of the Constitution: Student Workbook
Lessons of the Constitution: Parent /Teacher Resource

This volume is the workbook for a three part course of study on the United States Constitution. Written for home schools, private schools, family or personal study, the course offers in-depth understanding of our founding document. It can be used as independent or guided study for any age individual that reads comfortably.

Lessons of the Constitution: Student Workbook
Pamela Romney Openshaw
Copyrights by Openshaw Enterprises, LLC: 1st Edition © 2013; 2nd Edition © 2015
1st Printing: 2013; 2nd Printing: 2015; 3rd Printing: 2017

All rights reserved. No part of this book may be reproduced in any form or by any means without permission in writing from the publisher, Openshaw Enterprises.

For additional copies of the book, or information on other books and materials, contact:
Openshaw Enterprises
(801) 373-0240
openshawenterprises@gmail.com
www.promisesoftheconstitution.com

For special pricing on bulk purchases, or booking the author for a live event, contact:
Openshaw Enterprises
(801) 373-0240
openshawenterprises@gmail.com
www.promisesoftheconstitution.com

ISBN 978-0-9882550-5-0

Cover design by
Douglass Cole of Ninth Floor Design

General Edition
Printed in the United States of America by
Press Media, Provo, Utah 84604

Section One
WAITING

Introduction Activity

What do you believe about the beginnings of our country? Below is a series of statements about subjects that will be discussed in this section. In the left column, write "T" if you believe this statement is true, and write "F" if you believe this statement is false. Then complete the readings and questions in Section 1.

When you finish reading Section 1, reread these statements and answer them again, writing "T" or "F" in the column on the right. Are any of your answers different? Ponder what you learned while completing Section 1, and if any of your ideas and/or opinions have changed.

_____	All Americans wanted to be free from British government.	_____
_____	The Founding Fathers invented the idea that a government can be run by the people, for the people.	_____
_____	Running a government has nothing to do with morals, values, and religion.	_____
_____	True peace comes from within.	_____
_____	It was easier being an American in 1787 than it is today.	_____
_____	Freedom is something given to us by our government.	_____
_____	The United States government was inspired by teachings in the Bible.	_____

1.1 | America in June of 1787
"Bold, Fresh, Wild"

Be strong and of a good courage: for unto this people shalt thou divide for an inheritance the land, which I sware unto their fathers to give them.

— JOSHUA 1:6

1. In the space below, list three examples of how life in America in 1787 was different from today.

_____
_____
_____
_____

2. Describe, in one or two sentences, one way in which the American people were different from the British.

_____
_____
_____
_____

3. Would you have enjoyed living as an American in 1787? Explain why or why not in at least one paragraph.

_____
_____
_____
_____
_____
_____
_____

1.2 | A Pattern of Freedom
Setting Patterns

In all things shewing thyself a pattern of good works.

—Titus 2:7

1. This vignette is titled "A Pattern for Freedom." Where did the Founders find this pattern for freedom? Answer in complete sentences.

_____
_____
_____

2. Why do you think God cares about government? Explain your opinion in two or three sentences.

As governments have control over many facets of life it is my view that He cares about government because he cares about us. He also can us the gov to carry out his plan.

3. Here is a quote from this vignette: "Like other early settlers of America, many of the Founders governed their lives according to the 'Good Book.' Its pages gave them their basic education, their spirituality, and their common reason. Bible study guided their everyday actions and provided instruction and practical application in such matters as their use of time and the conduct of their relationships." Write one paragraph describing at least one way that the Bible has had an influence in the way you live your life.

_____
_____
_____
_____
_____
_____

1.3 | Announced, at Last
Confidence in the Face of Change

God is our refuge and strength, a very present help in trouble. Therefore will not we fear, though the earth be removed, and though the mountains be carried into the midst of the sea; Though the waters thereof roar and be troubled, though the mountains shake with the swelling thereof.
— Psalm 46:1–3

1. The men who drafted the Constitution were mostly "farmers, soldiers, merchants, lawyers, and landed gentry." How might the Constitution be different today if only men who were rich or who were royalty had created it? Explain your answer in one or two sentences.

_____
_____
_____
_____

2. The author writes that many other governments around the world were created "catch-as-catch-can." What does this phrase mean? If you don't know, look it up or ask an adult. Write the definition below in a complete sentence.

_____
_____
_____

3. Write a journal entry as if you were an American colonist the day the newspapers announced that the United States had a new government. What would you be excited about? What would you be concerned sabout? What would some of your biggest questions be?

_____
_____
_____
_____
_____
_____

1.4 | Freedom under the Constitution
Freedom

> *For, brethren, ye have been called unto liberty; only use not liberty for an occasion to the flesh, but by love serve one another.*
>
> — GALATIANS 5:13

1. An acrostic consists of a word that is written vertically. A word, short phrase, or sentence is then written horizontally next to each vertical letter. The word, phrase, or sentence written horizontally should begin with the letter it is written next to and must describe the vertical word. Complete the acrostic below for the word "freedom." The word, phrase, or sentence for each letter must describe what freedom is. For example, for the first letter in freedom, you could write, "Faiths and religions of all kinds are protected" next to the letter F.

2. How do we know that the founders of our country cared about freedom? Answer in one or two sentences.

_____
_____
_____

3. Think about five freedoms that you and your family enjoy. List them in the space below, beginning with the freedom that is most important to you.

The freedom of religion
The freedom of the press
The freedom of the pursuit of happyness
of speech and of life

1.5 | Protection under the Constitution
Protections

> *But whoso hearkeneth unto me shall dwell safely, and shall be quiet from fear of evil.*
> — PROVERBS 1:33

1. What does the word "inalienable" mean? If you don't know, look it up or ask an adult. Write the definition below in a complete sentence.

_____

_____

_____

2. Column A below lists rights that were denied to the people before the Constitution was written. Column B contains the protections that the Constitution promised. Match the letters from Column B with the numbers in Column A to show how the Constitution protected these violated rights.

COLUMN A

____1. The Government forbade citizens from worshipping with the religion of their choice.
____2. The Government could seize a person's property at will.
____3. Citizens could be imprisoned without a chance to prove their innocence.
____4. People could be punished for gathering in groups and speaking their minds in public areas.

COLUMN B

A. Citizens may publicly share their views and assemble as they please.
B. The people could practice their religious beliefs without being punished.
C. A person's belongings could not be taken without a lawful reason.
D. Everyone is entitled to a fair trial.

3. What kinds of protection do we enjoy today through the laws our country enforces? Identify at least two protections and write them below in a complete sentence.

_____

_____

_____

_____

1.6 Prosperity under the Constitution
Real Prosperity

Lay not up for yourselves treasures upon earth, where moth and rust doth corrupt, and where thieves break through and steal: But lay up for yourselves treasures in heaven, where neither moth nor rust doth corrupt, and where thieves do not break through nor steal: For where your treasure is, there will your heart be also.

— MATTHEW 6:19–21

1. Usually people think of wealth and riches when they think about prosperity. The author, however, talks about real prosperity as freedom, security, and happiness. Which kind of prosperity would you rather have: wealth and riches; or freedom, security, and happiness? Describe why in two or three sentences.

_____
_____
_____
_____
_____

2. Fill in the blanks for the following sentence from vignette 1.6 of the text: "Prosperity always results from the integrity of a nation's_____ and _____."

3. If a family enjoys real prosperity, does that mean they will not have adversity and trials? Explain why or why not in at least one paragraph.

No, because they will have access to prosperity and therefore have trials
_____
_____
_____
_____
_____

1.7 Peace under the Constitution
Peace

O that thou hadst hearkened to [the Lord's] commandments! Then had thy peace been as a river, and thy righteousness as the waves of the sea.

— Isaiah 48:18

1. In the space below, list three things that a government can do to help foster peace for its citizens.

2. In one paragraph, write about a particularly peaceful time or moment in your life. What was it like? What made it peaceful? What are the words that best describe that time for you?

Taking a nap was peaceful. It was quiet, not stressful, and relaxing.

3. What do you think the author means by "we must earn our peace"? Write at least one paragraph to explain your answer.

Section Two
PREPARING FOR FREEDOM

Introduction Activity

Section 2 explores the lives of America's early settlers, who paved the way for the United States to grow and flourish. There are many things you may know about the early pilgrims, settlers, and pioneers of this country. There are also many things that you may not know.

Below is a KWL chart. The "K" represents what you KNOW. Before reading Section 2, fill the "K" column with what you know about early American pilgrims, settlers, and pioneers. The "W" stands for what you WANT to know about them. Before reading Section 2, fill the "W" column with what you want or hope to learn about them. The "L" is what you LEARNED about them. Once you have completed all of Section 2, fill in the "L" column with things you have learned about early American pilgrims, settlers, and pioneers.

K What you KNOW	W What you WANT to know	L What you LEARNED

2.1 Settlers in America: Jamestown, 1607
The Dangers of Idleness

The way of the slothful man is as an hedge of thorns: but the way of the righteous is made plain.
— Prosverbs 15:19

1. Why did the settlers of Jamestown suffer from starvation? Write the answer below.

_____
_____
_____
_____

2. Imagine that you are one of the settlers of Jamestown. Even though you work hard all day, your neighbors who don't work at all get the same amount of food and supplies that you receive. How would you feel? Write those feelings below in at least two sentences.

_____
_____
_____
_____
_____

3. Write three negative consequences that come from being lazy. Then write three positive consequences that come from working hard. Use complete sentences.

_____
_____
_____
_____
_____
_____
_____
_____

2.2 | The Pilgrims of 1620: Christian Unity
A United Commitment to God

Two are better than one; because they have a good reward for their labour. For if they fall, the one will lift up his fellow: but woe to him that is alone when he falleth; for he hath not another to help him up. Again, if two lie together, then they have heat: but how can one be warm alone? And if one prevail against him, two shall withstand him; and a threefold cord is not quickly broken.

— ECCLESIASTES 4:9–12

1. The Pilgrims who settled in Plymouth wanted to "raise their children free from worldly influences." In the space below, list five worldly influences that can harm people today.

Trump, Joe (Not Joe Biden), Candice, China

2. How did Squanto help the Pilgrims in Plymouth? Write down at least two examples.

3. Imagine that you are a Jamestown settler who has come to visit a Pilgrim friend in Plymouth. In the space below, write a letter back home, telling your family how the Pilgrims in Plymouth are different from the settlers in Jamestown.

2.3 Arrival of the Puritans in 1630
A Covenant People

I the Lord have called thee in righteousness, and will hold thine hand, and will keep thee, and give thee for a covenant of the people, for a light of the Gentiles.

— Isaiah 42:6

1. What does it mean for someone to be a "light on a hill"? If you aren't sure, ask an adult, and then write down the meaning below.

_____
_____
_____

2. Circle the correct answer: Because the Puritan settlers in Boston tried hard to follow God, they did not suffer or have to go through hardships.
   True   False

3. A covenant is a sacred promise, often between men and God. What do you think it means that the Puritans were a "covenant people"? Write your explanation below.

_____
_____
_____
_____
_____
_____
_____

2.4 | John Winthrop, the "Puritan Moses"
Single-Mindedness

With my whole heart have I sought thee: O let me not wander from thy commandments.
— Psalm 119:10

1. John Winthrop was a man "who dressed in common clothing despite his wealth." What does this statement tell you about John Winthrop's character? Answer in one or two sentences.

_____
_____
_____
_____

2. When the food supplies were almost gone and the Lyon had not yet arrived, John Winthrop set aside a day of fasting. Why do you think he did this, instead of reacting with fear? Explain below in one or two sentences.

_____
_____
_____
_____

3. In two sentences, write down the biggest reason why you think John Winthrop was a great leader for the Puritans.

_____
_____
_____
_____

2.5 | Life among the Puritans
Laughter

A merry heart doeth good like a medicine.
— PROVERBS 17:22

1. Why do you think the scripture from Proverbs tells us that a merry heart is "like a medicine"? Explain below in at least two sentences.

_____
_____
_____

2. We have the stories in this vignette because the Puritans were faithful in keeping personal journals. Why do people keep journals? Write your answer below in one or two sentences.

_____
_____
_____

3. Write a story below about something funny that has happened in your family.

_____
_____
_____
_____
_____
_____
_____
_____
_____
_____
_____
_____

2.6 | The Puritans Receive Divine Assistance
Miracles

If ye have faith as a grain of mustard seed, ye shall say unto this mountain, Remove hence to yonder place; and it shall remove; and nothing shall be impossible unto you.

— MATTHEW 17:20

1. This vignette gives many examples of miracles. Which miracle story is your favorite, and why? Explain below in one paragraph.

_____

_____

_____

_____

_____

_____

2. In the last sentence of this vignette, the author writes, "God extends mercy to those who earnestly seek it." What can a person do to seek, or ask for, God's mercy? Answer in one or two sentences.

_____

_____

_____

3. In your opinion, do miracles happen today? What makes you think as you do? Explain your opinion below in at least three sentences.

_____

_____

_____

_____

_____

2.7 | George Whitefield and the Great Awakening, 1734

"Stir into Action"

Be thou an example of the believers, in word, in conversation, in charity, in spirit, in faith, in purity.
— 1 Timothy 4:12

1. This vignette contains lessons that George Whitefield taught to his listeners. Write one of them below.

___

2. How do you know that the early Americans cared deeply about religious worship? Explain in two or more sentences.

___

3. Do you believe that one person can influence others to change their lives? Explain your answer below, and then describe what you can do, right now, to influence someone's life for the better.

___

2.8 | British Oppression Builds
Resistance to Tyranny

> *Woe unto them that decree unrighteous decrees, and that write grievousness which they have prescribed.*
> — Isaiah 10:1

1. What is the definition of "tyranny"? If you don't know, look it up or ask an adult. Write the definition below in a complete sentence.

_____
_____

2. What was the final act of the British Parliament and King George III that made the American colonists rise in protest? Write the answer in a complete sentence below.

_____
_____

3. Imagine that you are living over two hundred years ago in the American colonies and you are writing a letter to a sympathetic friend living in Britain. In your letter, explain how you and the colonists feel about the oppression from the British government. Your letter should include at least one reference to a historical event from this period.

_____
_____
_____
_____
_____
_____
_____
_____
_____
_____
_____
_____

Section Three

CONFLICT AND INDEPENDENCE

Introduction Activity

The introductory page for Section 3 offers information that you need to know before reading Section 3. In the space below, please write a summary of the introduction. You may write the summary in a paragraph, or you may use bullet points.

3.1 | Samuel Adams, Flame of the Revolutionary Fire
Firmness of Purpose

Therefore, my beloved brethren, be ye stedfast, unmoveable, always abounding in the work of the Lord, forasmuch as ye know that your labour is not in vain in the Lord.

— 1 Corinthians 15:58

1. The word "unyielding" is used twice in reference to Samuel Adams. What does "unyielding" mean? If you don't know, look it up or ask an adult. Write the definition below in a complete sentence.

2. This vignette uses a lot of fire imagery (such as fire, flame, igniting, fanning the flames) when describing Samuel Adams and the work he did. Why do you think the author used these words to describe him? Write your answer in at least one sentence below.

3. We need both leaders and followers in our world. Leaders inspire and encourage others in a cause and help bring people together. Followers take action and lend their support for the cause they are working for. Are you a leader, a follower, or both? Write at least one paragraph explaining your answer.

Both, I can lead and support. I support sometimes and lead othertimes.

3.2 Rebellion Erupts
Pride

Only by pride cometh contention: but with the well advised is wisdom.

— Proverbs 13:10

1. The British government is described as being blind and deaf to the needs of the American colonists. How does pride make someone "blind" or "deaf"? Explain in one or two sentences.

_____
_____
_____
_____

2. Circle the best answer: The British tried to tax the American colonies by:

   a) forcing them to buy tea using British money.
   b) writing a law that said every citizen must pay 15 percent of his income to the British government.
   c) requiring that all business transactions carry a stamp purchased from the British.

3. At the famous Boston Tea Party of 1773, the colonists dumped all of the tea into the Boston harbor. Why? What message were they trying to send to Britain? Explain below in at least two sentences.

_____
_____
_____
_____
_____

3.3 | The Colonists Protest!
Teamwork

And let us consider one another to provoke unto love and to good works ... exhorting one another.
— HEBREWS 10:24–25

1. Circle the correct answer: The men did most of the protesting against the British, since they were the ones going to war and fighting.
   True   False

2. In your opinion, did the colonists protest because they were being selfish, or do you think it was for a different reason? Explain your opinion below in at least two sentences.

_____
_____
_____
_____
_____

3. This vignette gives many examples of the ways civilian colonists found a way to protest against the British or support the Continental Army in the Revolutionary War. Which example inspires you the most, and why? Explain below in one paragraph.

_____
_____
_____
_____
_____
_____
_____
_____

3.4 | The War for Independence Begins, 1775
Determination

Let us lay aside every weight . . . and let us run with patience the race that is set before us.
— HEBREWS 12:1

1. Although the Battle of Bunker Hill was a British victory, the British learned an important lesson about the Americans. What was it? Answer using at least one sentence.

_____
_____
_____

2. Write a journal entry as if you were Sam Whittemore. Describe why, if given the chance, you would fight the British soldiers again, despite your personal defeat and sacrifices.

_____
_____
_____
_____
_____
_____
_____

3. What do patience and determination have in common? How are they different? Explain your answer in one paragraph.

_____
_____
_____
_____
_____
_____
_____

3.5 | Finding a Commander
Qualified for the Job

Look not on his countenance, or on the height of his stature... for the Lord seeth not as man seeth; for man looketh on the outward appearance, but the Lord looketh on the heart.

— 1 Samuel 16:7

1. George Washington was unsure about his appointment as the American general leading the troops against the British. Describe an experience when you felt unsure, anxious, or inadequate about something you were expected to do.

2. What was it about George Washington that made him the perfect choice to serve as the American commander, in your opinion? Explain below in complete sentences.

3. Write one paragraph about the similarities between 1 Samuel 16:7, "Man looketh on the outward appearance, but the Lord looketh on the heart," and the popular saying, "Don't judge a book by its cover."

3.6 | George Washington, Revolutionary General
Leadership

> *Whosoever will be great among you, shall be your minister: And whosoever of you will be the chiefest, shall be servant of all. For even the Son of man came not to be ministered unto, but to minister, and to give his life a ransom for many.*
>
> — Mark 10:43-45

1. Thomas Jefferson said powerful things about Washington's abilities as a leader. Pick two characteristics mentioned that you like the best, and describe in one paragraph why they are meaningful to you.

_____
_____
_____
_____
_____
_____
_____

2. Circle the correct answer: Washington was not a natural military genius—he had to learn and adapt in order to fill his role as general.
   True   False

3. In the account narrated by the Indian chief, why do you think that God protected George Washington and guided him while he served his country? Explain in at least two sentences.

_____
_____
_____
_____
_____

3.7 | Writing the Declaration of Independence
Selfless Service

Serve him with a perfect heart and with a willing mind: for the Lord searcheth all hearts, and understandeth all the imaginations of the thoughts.

— 1 Chronicles 28:9

1. Writing and signing the Declaration of Independence was an act of service. Who were the Founding Fathers helping? Circle the best answer:

   a) Themselves
   b) Their families
   c) Future generations
   d) all of the above
   e) none of the above

2. As he lay dying, John Morton declared that signing the Declaration of Independence was "the most glorious service that I ever rendered my country." Why do you think he felt this way? Write your answer below.

_____
_____
_____

3. Describe a time when a family member, friend, acquaintance, or even a stranger performed an act of service for you. Include in your answer how you felt about that act of service and what you felt toward that person. Write at least one paragraph about this experience.

_____
_____
_____
_____
_____

3.8 | Thomas Jefferson, Author of the Declaration
Seeking after Knowledge

> *My son, if thou wilt receive my words . . . So that thou incline thine ear unto wisdom, and apply thine heart to understanding; Yea, if thou criest after knowledge, and liftest up thy voice for understanding; If thou seekest her as silver, and searchest for her as for hid treasures; Then shalt thou understand the fear of the Lord, and find the knowledge of God. For the Lord giveth wisdom: out of his mouth cometh knowledge and understanding.*
>
> — Proverbs 2:1–6

1. What is the difference between being smart and seeking after knowledge? Which is more important? Answer both of these questions below in complete sentences.

_____
_____
_____
_____
_____
_____

2. Even though Thomas Jefferson was not a part of the Constitutional Convention, he helped develop the ideas that would emerge in the Constitution. How did he do this?

_____
_____
_____
_____

3. Fill in the blanks with three sources from which a person can seek knowledge: "We can seek knowledge from_____ _____, and _____."

3.9 | The Finished Declaration
Acting on Faith

Now faith is the substance of things hoped for, the evidence of things not seen.
— HEBREWS 11:1

1. What is faith? If you don't know, look it up, ask an adult, or read the scripture for this vignette. Write the definition below in a complete sentence.

_____
_____

2. Henry Knox said that "As we play our part posterity will bless or curse us." How do you feel about the part our Founding Fathers played in our history? Why do you think some will bless them? Who do you think might curse them, and why? Answer these three questions in one paragraph.

_____
_____
_____
_____
_____
_____

3. Explain below, as if in a letter to a friend, how creating and publishing the Declaration of Independence was an enormous act of faith on the part of the Founding Fathers.

_____
_____
_____
_____
_____
_____
_____
_____

3.10 | John Adams, Voice of Freedom
Courage

> *Be strong and of a good courage, fear not, nor be afraid of them: for the Lord thy God, he it is that doth go with thee; he will not fail thee, nor forsake thee.*
>
> — Deuteronomy 31:6

1. Circle the correct answer: John Adams was very popular and was well liked by everyone.   True   False

2. Think of one example from this vignette that shows John Adams's courage, and write it below. Then explain how this is an example of courage.

_____
_____
_____
_____
_____

3. Describe one situation where you had to be courageous. How did you feel before, during, and after that situation was over? Write about this experience in one paragraph.

_____
_____
_____
_____
_____
_____
_____
_____
_____
_____
_____
_____

3.11 Embracing Independence
Life, Liberty, and Happiness

The Spirit of the Lord God is upon me; because the Lord hath anointed me to preach good tidings unto the meek . . . to proclaim liberty to the captives, and the opening of the prison to them that are bound.
— Isaiah 61:1

1. What does it mean to embrace something? If you don't know, look it up or ask an adult. Write the definition below in a complete sentence. Then explain why you think the author called this vignette "Embracing Independence."

_____

_____

_____

_____

2. John Adams declared that he was willing and ready to give everything he had, even his life, for independence and freedom. What things are so important to you that you would be willing to make some important sacrifices? Why? Write your answer below in at least three sentences.

_____

_____

_____

_____

_____

3. The delegates who signed the Declaration of Independence knew that if the Revolution failed, they would likely be killed. Why do you think they were willing to risk their lives in order to sign the Declaration?

_____

_____

_____

_____

3.12 | Ringing for Liberty
Rejoicing

> *But let all those that put their trust in thee rejoice: let them ever shout for joy, because thou defendest them.*
>
> — Psalm 5:11

1. Reread the poem found in this vignette. Using the space below, write as many words from the poem as you can that have to do with rejoicing, happiness, or excitement.

2. Today, the huge bronze bell—the Liberty Bell—is in Philadelphia near Independence Hall. Why do you think that our country still has the Liberty Bell today, instead of recycling it once it cracked?

_____
_____
_____
_____

3. Write about a time when you were so excited that you wanted to shout out the news to everyone! Tell in one paragraph what you were excited about, how you felt, and whom you told.

_____
_____
_____
_____
_____
_____
_____
_____

3.13 | The Miracle of Jefferson and Adams
Forgiveness

And be ye kind one to another, tenderhearted, forgiving one another, even as God for Christ's sake hath forgiven you.
— Ephesians 4:32

1. Circle the correct answer: On which day did both Jefferson and Adams die?
   a) July 4, 1826
   b) The fiftieth anniversary of the signing of the Declaration of Independence
   c) both a and b
   d) neither a nor b

2. Why do you think that God commands us to forgive one another? Explain below in at least one complete sentence.

___

3. Relate an experience when you either forgave someone or asked someone to forgive you. Why did you forgive or ask for forgiveness? How did you feel? Answer in one paragraph.

___

Section Four

WAR AND VICTORY!

Introduction Activity

Section 4 tells America's story, which includes the stories of many brave Americans who each played a part in America's Revolutionary War.

Below is a blank comic strip. First, read the introductory page for Section 4. Pay particular attention to the story of Peter Muhlenberg in the fourth paragraph. Then, use the blank comic strip below to tell the story of Peter Muhlenberg as described in the introduction. Be sure to draw and color pictures, as well as use dialogue and/or narration to tell his story.

4.1 | America versus Britain: David and Goliath
Fighting Goliath

Then said David to the Philistine, Thou comest to me with a sword, and with a spear, and with a shield: but I come to thee in the name of the Lord of hosts, the God of the armies of Israel, whom thou hast defied.

— 1 Samuel 17:45

1. In complete sentences, write at least two advantages the British forces had over the Continental Army.

_____
_____
_____
_____
_____

2. The author writes at the end of this vignette, "The Americans were stronger than they appeared." Where was their strength coming from? Write your answer using at least one sentence.

_____
_____
_____
_____

3. "Self-discipline" refers to the ability to control oneself. For example, it takes self-discipline not to make a hurtful comment to someone who has just been unkind to you. Write down at least one benefit of exercising self-discipline in your life.

_____
_____
_____
_____
_____

4.2 | Miracle of the Cannon, 1776
"Small Things Accomplish Great Events"

Behold, we put bits in the horses' mouths, that they may obey us; and we turn about their whole body. Behold also the ships, which though they be so great, and are driven of fierce winds, yet are they turned about with a very small helm, whithersoever the governor listeth. Even so the tongue is a little member, and boasteth great things. Behold, how great a matter a little fire kindleth!

—James 3:3–5

1. In the space below, write a short poem (four lines or more) that describes Henry Knox's amazing delivery of the artillery to General Washington. Try to make the poem rhyme.

2. Henry Knox did not let "winter weather and three hundred miles of rivers, lakes, and mountains" keep him from fulfilling his goal. He can be an example to us. Write down a goal that you have and the obstacles that might get in the way of achieving that goal. Then explain in at least two sentences what you plan to do to overcome those obstacles in order to meet your goal.

_____
_____
_____
_____
_____
_____

3. Circle the best answer: Which of the following was the great miracle of the cannon?
   a) Henry Knox and his men transported heavy artillery and cannons hundreds of miles in rough terrain.
   b) The American soldiers discovered a new strength after having endured the physical ordeal of Knox's trek.
   c) both a and b
   d) neither a nor b

4.3 | The Battle for Boston, 1776
Achieving Difficult Things with God's Help

With men this is impossible; but with God all things are possible.
— MATTHEW 19:26

1. The man who presented the idea of the French chandelier fortifications to General Washington was a junior officer, not an expert. What lesson can we learn from this young officer's experience? Explain in at least one complete sentence.

_____
_____
_____
_____

2. How did God make the task of fortifying Dorchester Hill possible? Write your answer below using complete sentences.

_____
_____
_____
_____
_____

3. In at least two complete sentences, write down an experience when you had to accomplish something that was seemingly impossible but were able to do it with God's help.

_____
_____
_____
_____
_____
_____
_____
_____

4.4 | The Miracle on Long Island, August 1776
God Directs Our World

Thine, O Lord, is the greatness, and the power, and the glory, and the victory, and the majesty: for all that is in the heaven and in the earth is thine; thine is the kingdom, O Lord, and thou art exalted as head above all.

— 1 Chronicles 29:11

1. General Washington promised that victory would come if Providence (God) was involved. Does General Washington's comment apply to all kinds of victories? If so, what does this tell us about how we should live our lives and plan for our futures? Your answers should total at least two sentences.

_____
_____
_____
_____
_____
_____

2. Circle the correct answer: Even though God performs miracles, He still expects us to do everything we can to help ourselves.   True   False

3. How does the knowledge that God watches over us make you feel? Write about it in at least three sentences.

_____
_____
_____
_____
_____
_____
_____
_____
_____
_____

4.5 | The Miracles at Trenton and Princeton, 1776
Fasting and Prayer

Turn ye even to me with all your heart, and with fasting.
— Joel 2:12

1. Read the scripture for this vignette. What do you think it means to turn to God with all of your heart, as opposed to with just a part of your heart? Explain below in two or three sentences.

_____
_____
_____
_____
_____

2. Explain how the American people "turned to God" in this vignette, using complete sentences.

_____
_____
_____

3. Write about an instance when you prayed or fasted for something in particular. How did God give you an answer? Describe what happened in one paragraph.

_____
_____
_____
_____
_____
_____
_____
_____

4.6 | Valley Forge: Crucible of Freedom, 1777
"The Refiner's Fire"

And he shall sit as a refiner and purifier of silver: and he shall purify the sons of Levi, and purge them as gold and silver, that they may offer unto the Lord an offering in righteousness.
— MALACHI 3:3

1. Explain in one or two sentences why the Continental Army did not receive the supplies they needed at Valley Forge.

_____
_____
_____

2. Do you think God knew or cared about the Continental Army during the winter at Valley Forge? Write your opinion below in one paragraph.

_____
_____
_____
_____
_____
_____

3. A refiner's fire is meant to make a substance (like metal) stronger and more pure. How could the winter at Valley Forge have made Washington's troops stronger and more pure, even though they were physically weak? Explain your answer in two or three sentences.

_____
_____
_____
_____
_____
_____
_____

4.7 | Miraculous River Crossings, 1781
The Power of Example

Young men likewise exhort to be sober minded. In all things shewing thyself a pattern of good works: in doctrine shewing uncorruptness, gravity, sincerity; Sound speech, that cannot be condemned; that he that is of the contrary part may be ashamed, having no evil thing to say of you.

— Titus 2:6–8

1. George Washington set a good example for his men by using clean language. Who in your life has set a good example for you? Describe this person and include the following: How do you know him or her? Why do you admire this person? Answer below in at least one paragraph.

_____
_____
_____
_____
_____
_____

2. Fill in the blanks in the following sentences from vignette 4.7: "Again and again, _____ sent the Continental Army a means to escape. His aid came in part because of the _____ of America's men."

3. Write a journal entry as if you were a soldier sitting at the table when George Washington made his remark about using clean language. Write down how you felt on that occasion.

_____
_____
_____
_____
_____
_____
_____

4.8 | British Surrender at Yorktown, 1781
Don't Give Up

And let us not be weary in well doing: for in due season we shall reap, if we faint not.
— GALATIANS 6:9

1. Circle the correct answer: The American troops never gave up because they had never lost a battle.   True   False

2. Another word to describe not giving up is "tenacity." Describe a time when you showed tenacity—when you wanted to give up but didn't. How did you feel when the experience was over? Write your answer in one paragraph.

_____
_____
_____
_____
_____
_____
_____
_____
_____
_____

3. When talking about the Battle of Yorktown in later years, to whom would General Washington always give credit for their victory? Write down what we learn about Washington from this. Your answer should be at least two sentences.

_____
_____
_____
_____

4.9 | The Failure of Offensive War
The Need for Wise Counsel

Every purpose is established by counsel: and with good advice make war.
— PROVERBS 20:18

1. Why didn't God help the American troops that attacked the British in Quebec, Canada? Write your answer below.

_____
_____
_____
_____

2. Circle the best answer: We can see that God's hand was absent in the American attempt to conquer British Canada because:

　a) the element of surprise was destroyed.
　b) the weather refused to cooperate.
　c) the men became lost.
　d) most of the American officers were killed.
　e) all of the above.

3. The scripture for this vignette counsels men to take "good advice." In your opinion, whose advice should you seek when you are thinking about an important decision? Why? Explain below in at least two sentences.

_____
_____
_____
_____
_____
_____

4.10 | The General Retires
Brotherly Love

Greater love hath no man than this, that a man lay down his life for his friends.
— JOHN 15:13

1. How can you tell that George Washington loved the men who served with him in the Revolutionary War? Write about two or more examples that show this brotherly love.

_____
_____
_____
_____
_____

2. Washington was offered a salary for his public duties in the fight for freedom, but he declined. Write one way that Americans today can show their gratitude to Washington for his unpaid service to our country.

_____
_____
_____

3. The scripture for this vignette tells of a brotherly love so strong that a man would "lay down his life for his friends." Although Washington did not die while in the service of his country, how could one argue that he still laid down his life for his friends? Explain your answer.

_____
_____
_____
_____
_____

Section Five

WRITING THE CHARTER OF FREEDOM

Introduction Activity

How much do you know about how the United States Constitution was written? Where did its ideas come from? Who wrote it? In the concept map below, the U.S. Constitution is at the center. On the solid lines, write down what you already know about the Constitution. Leave the dotted lines blank.

When you have completed Section 5, look at the concept map again and compare it to what you learned after the readings and questions for this section. On the dotted lines, write three new things that you learned about the Constitution from Section 5.

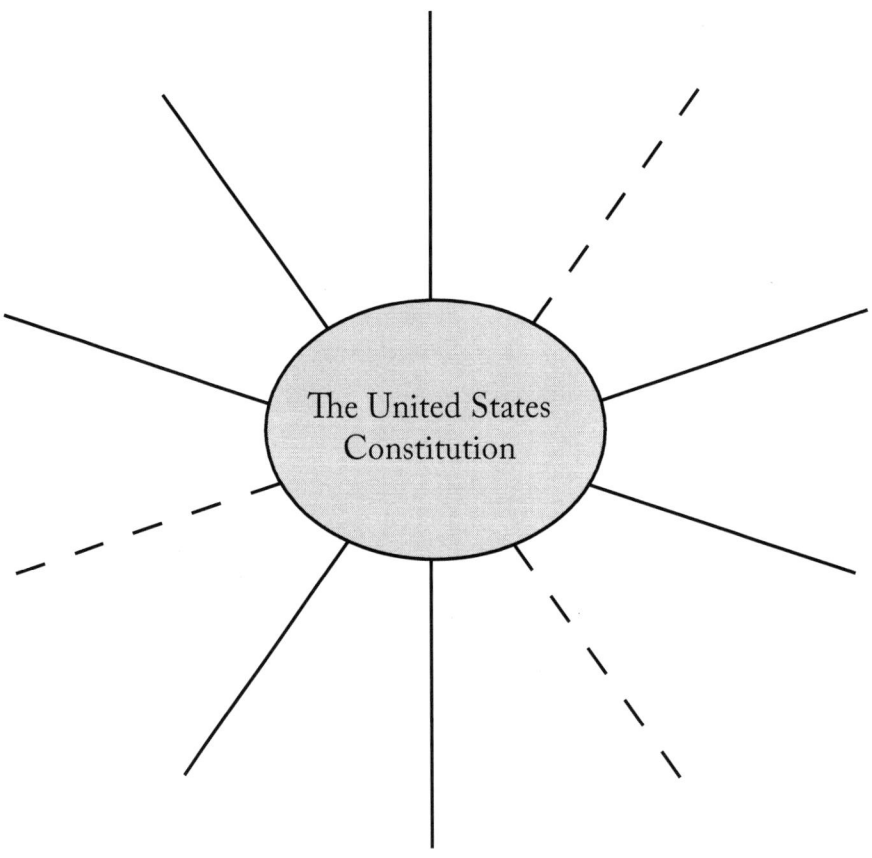

5.1 | The Articles of Confederation
Civil Obedience

> *Submit yourselves to every ordinance of man for the Lord's sake... For so is the will of God, that with well doing ye may put to silence the ignorance of foolish men: As free, and not using your liberty for a cloak of maliciousness, but as the servants of God.*
> — 1 Peter 2:13, 15–16

1. Write down one reason why the Articles of Confederation were ineffective.

_____
_____
_____
_____

2. The scripture for this vignette warns against using liberty as a "cloak" for wrongdoing. What is one example of the states abusing their liberty under the Articles of Confederation?

_____
_____
_____
_____

3. In one paragraph, describe the importance of obeying the laws in our country.

_____
_____
_____
_____
_____
_____
_____
_____

5.2 | Verging on Economic Collapse
Monetary Stability

Be thou diligent to know the state of thy flocks, and look well to thy herds. For riches are not for ever.
— PROVERBS 27:23–24

1. The United States had only two ways to pay for the war they had just won, since they had very little money. What were those options, and which did they choose?

_____
_____
_____
_____
_____
_____

2. Circle the correct answer: Taxes can be beneficial for our country and people if:

   a) taxes are kept minimal.
   b) the people approve them.
   c) the tax money is used wisely for all of the people.
   d) all of the above

3. What actions are available to you, as a young person, to help your family maintain stable finances? Brainstorm at least two ideas in a list below.

5.3 | The States Agree to Meet
Coming to Agreement

> *Now I beseech you, brethren, by the name of our Lord Jesus Christ, that ye all speak the same thing, and that there be no divisions among you; but that ye be perfectly joined together in the same mind and in the same judgment.*
>
> — 1 Corinthians 1:10

1. Circle the best answer: Why was it so important that delegates from each state agree to attend the Convention?
    a) The Convention could not meet without representation from each state.
    b) This would enable the delegates to all work together and create a Constitution that everyone could agree with.
    c) George Washington would not go unless everyone was there.
    d) none of the above

2. Circle the correct answer: You don't have to have the same opinions as everyone else in order to come to an agreement.   True   False

3. What benefits come from compromising (working together and putting aside differences)? Explain this below as if you were writing a letter to a friend with whom you have had a disagreement.

_____
_____
_____
_____
_____
_____
_____
_____
_____
_____
_____
_____

5.4 | James Madison, Father of the Constitution
Reasoning Together

> *And be not conformed to this world: but be ye transformed by the renewing of your mind, that ye may prove what is that good, and acceptable, and perfect, will of God.*
>
> — ROMANS 12:2

1. Fill in the blanks of this sentence from the vignette: "His [Madison's] ability to reason was based on_____ and _____ _____."

2. What did James Madison do daily to prepare for logical decisions during the Constitutional Convention? Write the answer below.

3. This vignette's scripture advises us to renew our minds. What do you think this means? Why do you think it would be important? Answer both questions below in at least one paragraph.

5.5 The Miracle at Philadelphia
Forbearance

Walk worthy of the vocation wherewith ye are called; With all lowliness and meekness, with longsuffering, forbearing one another in love; Endeavouring to keep the unity of the Spirit in the bond of peace.

— EPHESIANS 4:1–3

1. What is the definition of forbearance? If you don't know, look it up or ask an adult. Write the definition below in a complete sentence.

_____
_____

2. Write down one way in which the delegates would need to practice forbearance during the Constitutional Convention.

_____
_____
_____
_____
_____

3. What is the difference between putting up with each other and "forbearing one another in love," as the scripture above commands? Explain below in at least two sentences.

_____
_____
_____
_____
_____
_____
_____
_____

5.6 | Setting the Rules
Keeping Confidences

A talebearer revealeth secrets: but he that is of a faithful spirit concealeth the matter.

— PROVERBS 11:13

1. What do you think would have happened if there were no rules established for the Constitutional Convention? Write your answer in at least two sentences.

_____
_____
_____
_____
_____

2. Choose the best answer: Why do you think the Founding Fathers thought it was important to keep the details of the Constitutional Convention private?
   a) They didn't want the people to have a say in how the Constitution should be written.
   b) They wanted all the glory for themselves.
   c) They didn't want false rumors to be spread about what they were doing.
   d) They wanted the Constitution to be a surprise.

3. Respond to the following scenario about gossip: Imagine that someone you know was suddenly absent from school for two weeks. After a few days, other people in your class start to spread rumors about why this person is gone—he was suspended from school, got caught doing something he should not do, or is purposely skipping school. What should you do? Explain below in at least two sentences.

_____
_____
_____
_____
_____

5.7 | Men of the Constitution
Strengths and Weaknesses

And he said unto me, My grace is sufficient for thee: for my strength is made perfect in weakness. Most gladly therefore will I rather glory in my infirmities, that the power of Christ may rest upon me.

— 2 Corinthians 12:9

1. Circle the correct answer: The men who chose not to sign the Constitution were irresponsible.   True   False

2. What good can come from having weaknesses? Explain your answer in one paragraph.

___

3. Write down one weakness that you would like to overcome, and explain how you can overcome this weakness. Be sure to answer in complete sentences.

___

5.8 | Two Plans—and a Third
Remember Lessons of the Past

As a dog returneth to his vomit, so a fool returneth to his folly.
— Proverbs 26:11

1. Fill in the blanks with the correct answers: While debating how the government was to be organized, two plans were originally put forth. The first, from the Virginia Resolves, suggested that government power come from _____. The second, the New Jersey Plan, wanted the government's power to come from _____.

2. Why did no one support Alexander Hamilton's plan? Write the answer below.

3. Think of an instance when you learned from a mistake. What did you learn, and why is that particular lesson so memorable for you? Write about this experience in one paragraph.

5.9 The Great Compromise
Compromise

> *Can two walk together, except they be agreed?*
> — Amos 3:3

1. Choose the correct answer: How did the large and small states come to a compromise regarding how their states would be represented in Congress?

   a) They created two branches of Congress, with one branch representing the states according to their population and the other giving each state equal representation.
   b) They decided to have five representatives from each state, regardless of the population of that state.
   c) They eliminated the need for a Congress and established the role of a president.

2. Roger Sherman, who proposed the Great Compromise, presented the idea to the Convention three times before it was accepted. What lesson can Sherman's example teach us? Explain your answer in complete sentences.

_____
_____
_____

3. Write a journal entry about a time when you had to compromise with someone else. Describe the situation and how you worked together to come to an agreement. What did you learn from the experience?

_____
_____
_____
_____
_____
_____
_____
_____
_____
_____

5.10 | What about a President?
Using Power Wisely

> *Feed the flock of God which is among you, taking the oversight thereof, not by constraint, but willingly; not for filthy lucre, but of a ready mind; Neither as being lords over God's heritage, but being ensamples to the flock.*
>
> — 1 Peter 5:2–3

1. Circle the correct answer: Power is a bad thing to give to a person.
   True   False

2. Why did many delegates originally oppose James Wilson's idea of having a single person preside over the government? Write your answer below.

_____

_____

_____

_____

3. Create an acrostic using the word "power" (read the workbook page for vignette 1.4, question one, for instructions on how to create an acrostic). When writing the words, phrases, or sentences next to each letter, make sure that they all emphasize positive ways to use power.

5.11 | Admitting New Territories
Embracing Growth

Enlarge the place of thy tent, and let them stretch forth the curtains of thine habitations: spare not, lengthen thy cords, and strengthen thy stakes; For thou shalt break forth on the right hand and on the left . . . and make the desolate cities to be inhabited.

— Isaiah 54:2–3

1. Choose the incorrect answer out of the choices: Why did James Wilson advocate for admitting new states and giving them the same rights as the original thirteen?

    a) He feared that new states admitted with lesser rights would grow jealous.
    b) He didn't like the thirteen colonies the way they were at the time.
    c) He feared that the original and new states would separate from each other, potentially causing war.

2. Because the United States allowed western expansion, new opportunities were available to families who were ambitious and willing to work hard. In what ways can you benefit from working hard in today's world? In the space below, create a list of four benefits that come from hard work.

3. Change and growth often require a lot of work and can sometimes be intimidating. But positive change and growth are always rewarding. Describe, in one paragraph, a time when you experienced a change and became a better or stronger person because of it.

5.12 | Finishing the Document
Talents

Let your light so shine before men, that they may see your good works, and glorify your Father which is in heaven.
— Matthew 5:16

1. Select one man mentioned in this vignette and describe which of his talents he used to help finish writing the Constitution. Write in complete sentences.

_____
_____
_____
_____

2. What talent(s) do you have? Describe a situation where you have used a talent to benefit, serve, or help others.

_____
_____
_____
_____
_____

3. How does using our talents "glorify" God, as the scripture for this vignette asks us to do? Answer in at least two sentences.

_____
_____
_____
_____
_____
_____
_____

5.13 | Benjamin Franklin
Offering Public Service

For though I be free from all men, yet have I made myself servant unto all, that I might gain the more.
— 1 Corinthians 9:19

1. List two countries (other than the United States) that Benjamin Franklin traveled to in order to serve his country.

2. Franklin served his fellow men not only through politics, but also through his creative inventions. In the list below, circle the ways in which Franklin contributed to the good of the country and/or mankind.

- Invented the Internet
- Created bifocal eyeglasses
- Discovered a new planet
- Invented the glass harmonica
- Developed the first fire insurance company in America
- Found the origin of the common cold
- Discovered a cure for warts
- Described sunspots
- Created the first love potion
- Observed magnetic attraction
- Organized an expedition to the Arctic

3. What are some ways a person your age could serve his country now? List your ideas below.

5.14 Signatures and a Bill of Rights
Supporting Each Other

Fulfill ye my joy, that ye be likeminded, having the same love, being of one accord, of one mind.
— PHILIPPIANS 2:2

1. What did a delegate's signature on the Constitution represent? Explain below in one or two sentences.

_____
_____
_____

2. Benjamin Franklin expressed his support of the Constitution despite voicing many objections during the Convention. Why was it important that he support the group effort despite his feelings? Why was it important that he keep his feelings private? Answer in at least three sentences.

_____
_____
_____
_____
_____

3. Imagine that you are one of the Founding Fathers—how do you feel after writing and signing the Constitution? Write a letter home to your family to explain your feelings.

_____
_____
_____
_____
_____
_____

Section Six

THE FIGHT FOR RATIFICATION

Introduction Activity

Early Americans had many questions about their new charter of freedom. First, read the introductory page for Section 6. Then, create and write in the space below three questions that you have about the Constitution being approved, or ratified, by the thirteen colonies.

After you have completed the Section 6 readings and questions, come back to these three questions you wrote and, if you can, answer them. If you still do not know the answers, do some research and find those answers (using the internet, library books, and asking a parent or teacher).

1.

2.

3.

6.1 | The Federalist Papers
The Importance of Clarity

Study to shew thyself approved unto God, a workman that needeth not to be ashamed, rightly dividing the word of truth.

— 2 Timothy 2:15

1. What was the purpose of the Federalist Papers? Write the answer below in complete sentences.

_____
_____
_____
_____

2. The Founding Fathers believed that an effective, fair government must be transparent. What does transparent mean? If you don't know, look it up or ask an adult. Write the definition below.

_____
_____

3. Many people feel that they do not know enough about how the United States government is run. How can people learn more about our government and their roles in it? Answer below in at least two sentences.

_____
_____
_____
_____
_____
_____
_____

6.2 In Pennsylvania
Overcoming Fear

Fear thou not; for I am with thee: be not dismayed; for I am thy God: I will strengthen thee; yea, I will help thee; yea, I will uphold thee with the right hand of my righteousness.

— Isaiah 41:10

1. Many people in Pennsylvania were afraid of supporting the Constitution and the new government. Put yourself in their shoes by writing a letter to a friend, as if you were an American colonist, discussing why you might have been afraid of the proposed change.

_____
_____
_____
_____
_____
_____

2. Imagine that you are James Wilson, the man who presented and argued for the Constitution during the Pennsylvania state ratification convention for five weeks. Write one journal entry describing your feelings while you struggle to relieve people's fears in Pennsylvania.

_____
_____
_____
_____
_____
_____

3. Write down one thing that a person can do to help overcome his fears.

_____
_____
_____

6.3 | In Massachusetts
"A Time to Sow and a Time to Reap"

For whatsoever a man soweth, that shall he also reap.

— GALATIANS 6:7

1. The Antifederalists in Massachusetts are described as "ill managed, wordy, and excitable," whereas the Federalists were "logical, organized, and respectful of all opinions." In your opinion, which of these is the best way to accomplish a task? Explain why in at least three sentences.

_____
_____
_____
_____
_____

2. What was Jonathan Smith, the farmer, talking about when he said that "now is the time to reap the fruit of our labor?" Explain your answer in at least two sentences.

_____
_____
_____
_____
_____

3. Why do you think Samuel Adams's role in Massachusetts was so important in ratifying the Constitution? Answer in complete sentences.

_____
_____
_____
_____

6.4 In Virginia
Submitting to Authority

Let every soul be subject unto the higher powers. For there is no power but of God: the powers that be are ordained of God.

— ROMANS 13:1

1. Choose the best answer: "Patrick Henry was a man known for his_____ _____."

   a) cautious nature
   b) cowardice
   c) calm reasoning skills
   d) passionate emotions

2. Patrick Henry, upon finding out that Virginia would ratify the Constitution against his wishes, submitted to authority and sent the angry crowds home. In two or three sentences, explain your feelings about Patrick Henry's great strength of character in supporting the political process and its leaders.

   _____
   _____
   _____
   _____
   _____
   _____
   _____

3. Circle the correct answer: Each person, of whatever age or station in life, has it within his power to be an influence for good or evil.
   True   False

6.5 Waiting and Celebration
Blessings through Trials

For I reckon that the sufferings of this present time are not worthy to be compared with the glory which shall be revealed.

— ROMANS 8:18

1. What do you think was one of the difficult trials for the Founding Fathers in forming their new government? How did the Founders solve this problem or get through this particular trial? Write your answers below in at least two sentences.

_____
_____
_____
_____

2. Imagine that you are one of the Founding Fathers. A newspaper reporter is interviewing you and asks, "If you had to repeat the process of writing the Constitution and ratifying it, would you do it again, even if it meant repeating the arguments, trials, and difficult times?" Answer below in the form of an interview response.

_____
_____
_____
_____
_____
_____

3. Blessings can come through trials, depending on how the person responds to those trials. What can you do to receive the blessings that can come from trials?

_____
_____

Section Seven

BASIC GOVERNING PRINCIPLES

Introduction Activity

The crossword puzzle below contains words that are important in understanding the concepts and ideas in Section 7. Before reading this section, complete the crossword puzzle.

```
S E S B H V R P R U O R H Q X S R T K K
O E C T S C A E S S O I T T R E E N N Q
B Z C I A T E E L N O T O E Q V S E V E
U U B N T T P E O I N P W T E L P M L R
I N Y E A S E H P H G O G R P N O N Q I
F E R F L L U G Y S P I T G M I N R L M
Y N W G C H A J O L E I O Y J L S E P U
S G X F C X M B A V C E T N F D I V V Q
T C E T O R P T D A E I R Z I D B O T S
I N B Y Z K N I L N L R Q F V P I G N E
U O P V U O U P G A A A N C P A L L I L
E H J X Z G O Y U S B S P M U W I A A F
S H A I M W G Q A F F N K A E B T R R R
E J R M E T E C Q V K C A C U N Y E T U
Q O O R N M O R A L I T Y B E R T D S L
H D S E L B A N E I L A N I A H E E E E
R E P R E S E N T A T I V E S X C F R K
K B L Z G Z O L D U T Y X E T R I A T P
P B I C S A A Q P F Y R E L Q L O O M A
B V P H O M M M U O J X R S L Y V V V P
```

CHECKS AND BALANCES
DUTY
EQUALITY
FEDERAL GOVERNMENT
FREE SPEECH
HONOR
HORIZONTAL POWERS
INALIENABLE
JUSTICE
MORALITY

PATTERNS
PROTECT
RELIGION
REPRESENTATIVES
RESPONSIBILITY
RESTRAINT
SELF RULE
STATE GOVERNMENT
VERTICAL POWERS
VOICE

7.1 | Is the Constitution Outdated?
Using Power

Woe unto him that buildeth his house by unrighteousness, and his chambers by wrong; that useth his neighbour's service without wages, and giveth him not for his work.

— JEREMIAH 22:13

1. Circle the correct answer: It's acceptable for someone to use power to force people to do good things.　　True　　False

2. The Constitution put in place a system of checks and balances to distribute power among the separate branches of government. This ensures that each branch has limited power and authority in certain areas. Why did the Founders want to limit the amount of power that elected officials have in government? Answer in at least two sentences.

_____
_____
_____
_____

3. The Constitution is structured so that important actions (such as creating a new law) take considerable time. List at least two benefits that might come from taking your time in carrying out an important task.

7.2 | Rights, Duties, and Government
The Divine Origin of Rights

Know ye that the Lord he is God: it is he that hath made us, and not we ourselves; we are his people, and the sheep of his pasture.

— Psalm 100:3

1. Choose the correct answer: Which of the following is an example of a divinely given right?

    a) The right to make our own choices
    b) The right to be treated fairly
    c) The right to use the Earth's natural resources
    d) all of the above
    e) none of the above

2. Do people have to do something to earn or deserve an inalienable right? Explain why or why not in at least two sentences.

_____
_____
_____
_____
_____

3. The author asserts that with certain rights come certain duties. Write down two rights that you enjoy, and then write down what duties come along with enjoying those rights.

_____
_____
_____
_____
_____
_____
_____

7.3 Vertical Powers and Local Government
Being Heard

Take you wise men, and understanding, and known among your tribes, and I will make them rulers over you. And ye answered me, and said, The thing which thou hast spoken is good for us to do. So I took the chief of your tribes, wise men, and known, and made them heads over you, captains over thousands, and captains over hundreds, and captains over fifties, and captains over tens, and officers among your tribes.
— Deuteronomy 1:13–15

1. Below is a tree that represents the vertical powers the Founding Fathers wrote into the Constitution, patterned after God's example. Label each level with the appropriate representative groups: county, state, family, national government, and city. "A" is the first, most basic governing unit, and "E" is the most distant.

    e. _____
    c. _____   d. _____
    a. _____   b. _____

2. Match the duties in Column A with the appropriate leaders in Column B below.

    COLUMN B
    1. Responsible for budgeting one state's finances
    2. Vote on federal laws in Congress
    3. Discuss security with leaders of other countries
    4. Enforce traffic laws in one city

    COLUMN B
    a. City police force
    b. State Governor
    c. Senators and Representatives in national Congress
    d. President of the United States

3. Choose the best answer: Imagine you want to start a recycling program in your neighborhood. Who would be the best person to talk with in getting this program started?
    a) Your teacher
    b) One of your city officers
    c) The president of the United States

7.4 | Who Is in Charge: State versus Federal
Keeping Government Close

> *Now I beseech you, brethren, mark them which cause divisions and offences contrary to the doctrine which ye have learned; and avoid them. For they that are such serve not our Lord Jesus Christ, but their own belly; and by good words and fair speeches deceive the hearts of the simple.*
>
> — ROMANS 16:17–18

1. Choose the best answer: The Constitution set up the government so that:

   a) the federal government could tell the states what to do.
   b) the states could tell the federal government what to do.
   c) the states and the federal government could perform their own duties with little overlap.

2. Make a list of at least three responsibilities of the state governments in which the federal government shouldn't intervene.

3. Who is in the best position to make sure that your needs as a United States citizen are met: a state representative, or a federal representative? Explain your answer in two complete sentences.

BASIC GOVERNING PRINCIPLES

7.5 | Horizontal Powers
Dividing Power

> *Bear ye one another's burdens.*
> — GALATIANS 6:2

1. The federal government's power is divided into three branches. Under each branch labeled below, briefly write that branch's share of power or responsibility.

Legislative Branch
_____

Executive Branch   Judicial Branch
_____   _____

2. The author writes that the government's greatest responsibility is to "preserve freedom through four simple principles." All four of these principles deal with the citizens' duties in government. Why is it as important for citizens to have duties as it is for mayors, governors, senators, and the president? Explain in at least three sentences.

_____
_____
_____
_____
_____
_____

3. The family is the most basic unit of government. Describe in three to four sentences how a family is a form of government.

_____
_____
_____
_____
_____
_____

7.6 | Equality: What It Is and What It Isn't
Charity for Others

Every man according as he purposeth in his heart, so let him give; not grudgingly, or of necessity: for God loveth a cheerful giver.

— 2 Corinthians 9:7

1. Choose the correct answer: Equality means that everyone has the same things.   True   False

2. What does it mean to compel someone? If you don't know, look it up or ask an adult. Write the definition below.

_____
_____
_____

3. The author writes that God "instructs us to give freely to those in need." Create a list below of ways that you can give to those in need. Keep in mind that giving to the needy does not necessarily mean giving up your things or spending lots of money. Your list should include at least three ideas.

7.7 Freedom and Morality Intertwined
Knowing Right from Wrong

He that keepeth the law, happy is he.
— Proverbs 29:18

1. Circle the correct answers to fill in the blanks: "The more_____ (moral, popular) we are, the _____(more, less) law we need and the_____(more, less) free we are."

2. Why do moral people need fewer laws, and why do careless or thoughtless people need more laws? Explain your answer in two or three sentences below.

_____
_____
_____
_____
_____
_____

3. Imagine a world where everyone understands and chooses right over wrong and is free. Write a journal entry as if you lived in this kind of world and describe what a typical day in this world is like.

_____
_____
_____
_____
_____
_____
_____
_____
_____
_____
_____

7.8 | Separating Church and State
Acknowledge God

Blessed is the nation whose God is the Lord; and the people whom he hath chosen for his own inheritance.
— Psalm 33:12

1. Circle the correct answer: The "separation of church and state" is never mentioned in those words in the Declaration of Independence or the Constitution.   True   False

2. How do you think our country would be different today if public schools were permitted to teach about God, basic principles of religion, and morality? Write your opinion below in one paragraph.

_____
_____
_____
_____
_____
_____
_____
_____

3. Write at least one paragraph describing why God is the foundation of our government.

_____
_____
_____
_____
_____
_____
_____
_____

7.9 The Golden Rule in Government
Doing Good to Others

> *Therefore all things whatsoever ye would that men should do to you, do ye even so to them.*
> — Matthew 7:12

1. Choose the best answer: Which of the following demonstrates the appropriate way to practice the Golden Rule in government?
   a) Everyone gets the same things.
   b) Some people don't have to obey the laws because they hold important positions.
   c) Everyone has the same rights and liberties.
   d) Everyone is mostly equal.

2. On a scale of one to ten, how well do you think you live the Golden Rule? (One is "not at all," and ten is "all the time.") Write that number, and then write one thing you can change in your life to help you live the Golden Rule better.

_____
_____
_____
_____
_____

3. Do you think that if individual citizens practiced the Golden Rule, governments would be more likely to use the Golden Rule as well? Explain why or why not in two or three sentences.

_____
_____
_____
_____
_____
_____
_____

Section Eight

ECONOMIC FREEDOM

Introduction Activity

Section 8 focuses on defining sound economic principles. This activity will require one U.S. coin, such as a penny, nickel, dime, or quarter. Examine it, and draw the front of that coin into Circle 1 below. After reading the introductory page for Section 8, draw an additional coin. This time, create your own design for what an American coin could look like. Be sure to include the motto "In GOD we trust" and the word "LIBERTY," included on all U.S. coins, in your new design. Think of a principle, or truth, that would help guide America today toward greatness and prosperity; try to incorporate that into your new coin. Then, after completing all of Section 8, draw one more new coin design, using principles and truths that you learned in this section.

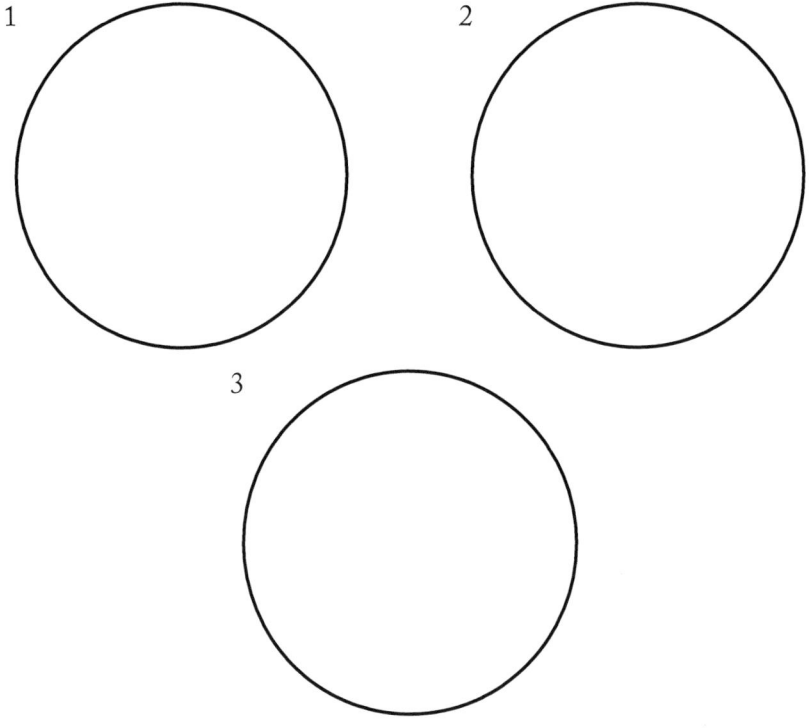

8.1 Appropriate Government in Economics
The Right to Choose

> *Choose you this day whom ye will serve.*
> — Joshua 24:15

1. Circle the correct answers to complete this sentence: "A free enterprise market _____ (encourages, discourages) competition and requires _____ (much, little) government intervention."

2. In one or two complete sentences, write at least one similarity between a government having control in the marketplace, and that same government controlling other rights, such as religion.

_____
_____
_____
_____
_____

3. A free market requires the right to try, to succeed, and even to fail. Explain, in at least one paragraph, why all of these rights are important in bringing products, or things to buy, to the marketplace.

_____
_____
_____
_____
_____
_____
_____
_____
_____
_____

8.2 | Owning Property
Stewardship over Property

And the Lord said, Who then is that faithful and wise steward, whom his lord shall make ruler over his household . . . ? Blessed is that servant, whom his lord when he cometh shall find so doing. Of a truth I say unto you, that he will make him ruler over all that he hath.

— Luke 12:42–44

1. What is another word for stewardship? If you don't know, look it up or ask an adult. Write the definition below.

_____
_____

2. Why do you think people work harder for the things they own or paid for with their own money? Explain in two or more sentences.

_____
_____
_____
_____
_____
_____

3. The scripture for this vignette asks for a "faithful and wise" steward, or manager. Create a list of at least three characteristics that you think are required to be a faithful and wise steward over something or someone.

8.3 | The Gold and Silver Standard
Things Are Not Always as They Appear

Beware of false prophets, which come to you in sheep's clothing, but inwardly they are ravening wolves.
— MATTHEW 7:15

1. In your own words, explain how currency, which began as precious metals, eventually became paper money. This summary should be at least two or three sentences.

_____
_____
_____
_____
_____

2. Choose the answer that is not true: The American dollar is not what it appears to be because:
   a) the dollar no longer represents a valuable item, like gold or silver.
   b) additional money can be printed at any time, even when the nation cannot afford it.
   c) printing more money gives us plenty of money, so the government has all it wants.

3. How would your life be different if no one accepted your money because they believed it was worthless? Could you eat the same foods, enjoy the same activities, and live in the same place if your money did not have value? Write three sentences that describe this scenario.

_____
_____
_____
_____
_____
_____
_____

8.4 | Inflation
Worth and Worthlessness

> *Go to now, ye rich men, weep and howl for your miseries that shall come upon you. Your riches are corrupted... Your gold and silver is cankered; and the rust of them shall be a witness against you.... Behold, the hire of the labourers who have reaped down your fields, which is of you kept back by fraud, crieth: and the cries of them which have reaped are entered into the ears of the Lord of sabaoth.*
>
> JAMES 5:1–4

1. Circle the correct answers to complete this sentence: "_____ (Inflation, Increased prices) is/are caused by _____ (inflation, increased prices)."

2. How is inflation, or the illusion of worth, similar to adding lots of water to juice? Explain in at least two sentences.

_____
_____
_____
_____
_____
_____

3. Explain in at least two sentences why printing more money without increasing goods or services to buy with the money does not give more wealth to the people of a nation.

_____
_____
_____
_____
_____
_____

Section Nine

— ◯ —

THE CONSTITUTION: MAKING THE LAWS

Introduction Activity

Section 9 explains the way the Constitution was written by the Founding Fathers, and then discusses how the Constitution has been changed. Below is a Venn diagram. In the left circle and right circle, you will write words or phrases that describe the differences between the Constitution in 1787 and the Constitution today. In the middle where the two circles meet, you will write words or phrases that describe the ways that the Constitution is the same today as it was when it was first written.

There are thirteen vignettes in this section. After completing each vignette, come back to this page and write one observation on the Venn diagram, either a similarity or a difference. When you have completed Section 9, you should have at least thirteen similarities and/or differences on the diagram.

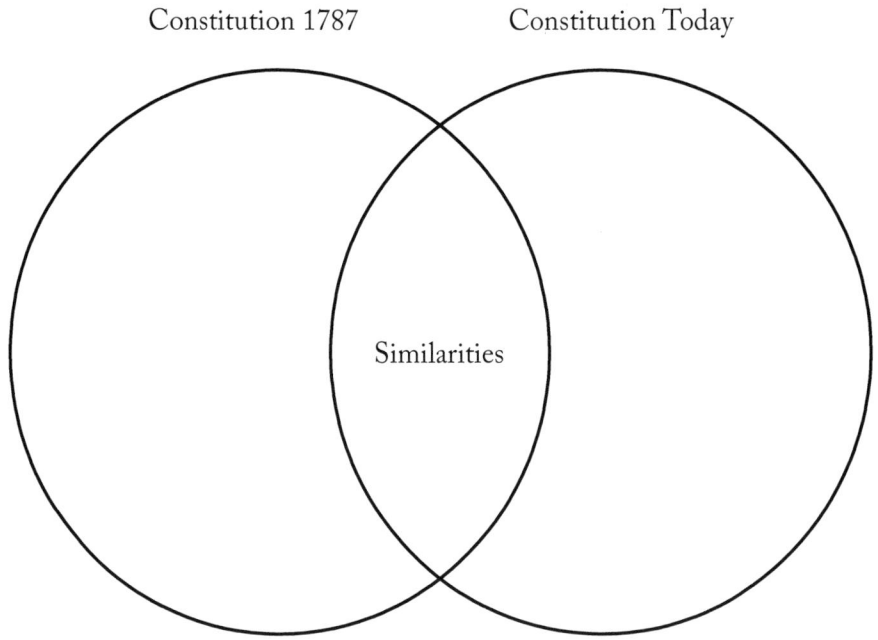

9.1 | The Preamble to the United States Constitution
Self-Government

> *Stand fast therefore in the liberty wherewith Christ hath made us free, and be not entangled again with the yoke of bondage.*
> — GALATIANS 5:1

1. Select the best answer to fill in the blank: "The Constitution defines the_____ as the source of power."

   a) president
   b) people
   c) government
   d) law

2. Laws are constitutionally created only through Congress (the House of Representatives and the Senate). If our elected representatives are the ones who actually create the laws, how is it that the people have an influence over the laws that are created and passed? Explain below in at least one sentence.

_____
_____
_____
_____

3. The author describes six claims to the right of self-government (which are found in the Preamble to the Constitution). Of those six, which is the most important to you personally, and why? Write one paragraph explaining your answer.

_____
_____
_____
_____
_____
_____
_____
_____

9.2 | The Brilliance of Balanced Government
Balance in Government

Law is good, if a man use it lawfully.

— 1 Timothy 1:8

1. Create an acrostic for the word "balance" (read the workbook page for vignette 1.4, question one, for instructions on how to create an acrostic).

2. Choose the best answer to fill in the blank: "The Constitution acknowledges that men tend to _____, so it puts roadblocks in place to prevent that from happening."

   a) usurp or draw power to themselves
   b) give up easily in the face of opposition
   c) be too generous with money they don't have

3. What do you think would happen if one branch had control over the entire government? Select one branch of government, and write one paragraph describing the misuse of power that might result if that branch had complete control.

_____
_____
_____
_____
_____
_____
_____
_____
_____
_____

9.3 | The House of Representatives
Representation as a Stewardship

It seemed good unto us, being assembled with one accord, to send chosen men unto you.

— Acts 15:25

1. Stewardship involves great responsibilities. Why is it important for a steward to be responsible? Explain your answer below in at least two sentences.

_____
_____
_____
_____
_____
_____

2. The term of office for members of the House of Representatives, which is the only branch that can initiate laws having to do with money, is only two years. Write at least one sentence explaining why.

_____
_____
_____

3. In at least one complete sentence, explain why there are so many more representatives serving in the House (435) than in the Senate (100).

_____
_____
_____
_____

9.4 | Slavery and the Three-Fifths Rule
All Are Created Equal

> *There is neither Jew nor Greek, there is neither bond nor free, there is neither male nor female: for ye are all one in Christ Jesus.*
>
> — GALATIANS 3:28

1. Choose the best answer: If each slave had received the same representation as a white person, what would have been the result in the House of Representatives?

   a) The House may have decided not to represent the Southern states.
   b) A state would be given less power because slaves weren't allowed to vote.
   c) A state would be given more power even though slaves weren't allowed to vote.

2. The manumission (freedom) of slaves was not written into the Constitution to become immediately effective because of complications. Write down two of those complications.

_____
_____
_____
_____
_____
_____
_____

3. The Constitution set 1808 as the deadline to end the importation (bringing) of slaves to the United States. Why, then, did emancipation not take place until sixty years later? Explain in one or two sentences.

_____
_____
_____
_____
_____

9.5 | The Senate Under the Original Constitution
Linking State and Federal

For as we have many members in one body, and all members have not the same office: So we, being many, are one body in Christ, and every one members one of another.

— ROMANS 12:4–5

1. Choose the best answer to fill in the blank: "The Constitution, as it was first written, states that members of the Senate are to be chosen by the_____."

   a) people
   b) state legislatures
   c) president of the United States

2. Write down two things that distinguish the Senate from the House of Representatives.

_____
_____
_____
_____

3. Explain in two or three sentences why it is important for government leaders, such as Senators, to "exercise sound judgment and be respectable, experienced, and mature."

_____
_____
_____
_____
_____
_____
_____

9.6 Upending the Constitution: The Seventeenth Amendment
The Consequences of Change

> *In transgressing and lying against the Lord, and departing away from our God . . . judgment is turned away backward, and justice standeth afar off: for truth is fallen in the street, and equity cannot enter. Yea, truth faileth.*
>
> — Isaiah 59:13–15

1. Which branch of Congress was affected by the Seventeenth Amendment, and what did the Seventeenth Amendment change? Write your answers below in complete sentences.

_____
_____
_____
_____

2. Part of the reason state governments lost their representation in Congress is that some state legislatures argued among themselves and never selected their Senators. What lesson could we learn from this unfortunate event? Explain below.

_____
_____
_____

3. The Seventeenth Amendment prevents state governments from having any representation (vote) in Congress. Describe in two sentences or more how you would feel if you were no longer allowed to vote in student, school, or any kind of elections. Would you think that is fair? Answer this question in the form of a journal entry.

_____
_____
_____
_____
_____

9.7 | What Congress Does: Taxation and the Sixteenth Amendment
Keeping What We Earn

He that earneth wages earneth wages to put it into a bag with holes.
— Haggai 1:6

1. Does the Sixteenth Amendment violate any of the freedoms described in the Preamble to the Constitution? Explain why or why not in two or three sentences.

_____
_____
_____
_____

2. Both the Constitution and the Sixteenth Amendment give national government the power to tax its people. One method is wise; one is not. In one paragraph, explain which is which and why the wise method works.

_____
_____
_____
_____
_____
_____

3. The scripture for this vignette uses the image of putting money into a bag with holes. In one or more sentences, describe how allowing the federal government to tax people for any reason (decided in the Butler ruling) is wasteful, like putting money into a bag with holes.

_____
_____
_____
_____

9.8 What Congress Does: Regulating Money
Greed

> *Thou hast taken usury and increase, and thou hast greedily gained of thy neighbours by extortion, and hast forgotten me, saith the Lord God.*
>
> — Ezekiel 22:12

1. Explain below the concept of interest charged on borrowed money (usury).

_____
_____
_____
_____
_____
_____

2. Select the two correct answers: The Federal Reserve Bank makes money "out of nothing" by:

    a) printing paper money without having valuables to back it up.
    b) charging interest on borrowed money.
    c) letting the federal government take its money.

3. Do you think is it appropriate to make money without having to work for it? Explain why or why not in one paragraph.

_____
_____
_____
_____
_____
_____
_____
_____
_____

9.9 | What Congress Does: Spending
Self-Sufficiency

Exact no more than that which is appointed you.

— Luke 3:13

1. Circle the correct answer: The government can generate (earn, not print) its own income.　　　True　　　False

2. Explain in at least two sentences how a government giving unwise financial assistance can harm not only those whose money it takes, but also those who receive the assistance.

_____
_____
_____
_____
_____
_____

3. Imagine that a family in your neighborhood is struggling to pay bills because the father is unemployed. You want to help. Would you give your own money to assist them? Would you have the right to take someone else's money if you were going to use it to help them? Explain your opinions in two sentences.

_____
_____
_____
_____
_____
_____
_____
_____

9.10 | What Congress Does: Borrowing and Bankruptcy
The Bondage of Debt

> *Render therefore to all their dues: tribute to whom tribute is due; custom to whom custom; fear to whom fear; honour to whom honour. Owe no man any thing, but to love one another: for he that loveth another hath fulfilled the law.*
>
> — ROMANS 13:7–8

1. The author describes debt as being "in bondage" or "in chains." Write down at least two other words or phrases that accurately describe being in debt.

_____
_____

2. What does it mean if a debt is "carried through the generations"? Explain below.

_____
_____
_____
_____
_____

3. Write down two strategies you can use to save and use money wisely.

_____
_____
_____
_____
_____
_____
_____
_____
_____

9.11 | What Congress Does: The Hotly Contested Commerce Clause
Oppressive Rules

Study to be quiet, and to do your own business, and to work with your own hands.
— 1 Thessalonians 4:11

1. Circle the correct answers to fill in the blanks: "The commerce clause in the Constitution allows federal involvement only in trade with_____ _____ (other nations, local businesses) and _____ (Congress, among the states)."

2. Rules are a good thing when used appropriately. Explain in two sentences how too many rules can be a problem.

_____
_____
_____
_____
_____
_____

3. Describe in one paragraph how the expanded commerce clause became oppressive for businesses.

_____
_____
_____
_____
_____
_____
_____
_____
_____
_____
_____

9.12 | What Congress Does: War Powers and National Lands
Taking Advantage of Others

Righteousness exalteth a nation: but sin is a reproach to any people.
— Proverbs 14:34

1. Circle the correct answer: In order to join or declare a war, the entire population of the United States has to agree to it.   True   False

2. If the federal government were to give all "federal-owned" lands back to the states, how would the states benefit financially? Explain in at least one complete sentence.

_____
_____
_____
_____
_____
_____

3. Make a list of at least two things a state could do if it owned more land within its boundaries.

9.13 | What Congress and the States Cannot Do
Fairness

Put them in mind to be subject to principalities and powers, to obey magistrates, to be ready to every good work.
— Titus 3:1

1. This vignette provides many examples of how the Constitution the Founding Fathers wrote strives for fairness for its citizens. Write down one of these examples below.

_____
_____
_____
_____
_____

2. Write down your definition of fairness. Explain your answer below.

_____
_____
_____
_____

3. Why it is wise to encourage fairness in the nation but not acceptable to force everyone to have equal things? Explain below in at least three sentences.

_____
_____
_____
_____
_____
_____
_____

Section Ten

THE CONSTITUTION: ENFORCING AND INTERPRETING THE LAW

Introduction Activity

Below is a series of statements about subjects that will be discussed in this section. In the left column, write "T" if you believe this statement is true, and write "F" if you believe this statement is false. Then complete the readings and questions in Section 10.

When you finish reading Section 10, reread these statements and answer them again, writing "T" or "F" in the column on the right. Are any of your answers different? Ponder about what you learned while completing Section 10, and how any of your ideas and/or opinions have changed.

_____	The President of the United States should serve the people in his country.	_____
_____	The President represents all Americans to the rest of the world.	_____
_____	Judges can make rulings based on their opinions.	_____
_____	The President is voted into office the way the Founding Fathers intended.	_____
_____	Juries should never be able to ignore laws.	_____
_____	Changing the Constitution is always bad.	_____
_____	Changing the Constitution is always good.	_____
_____	All the States must follow all the same laws.	_____

10.1 | What the President Does
Too Many Burdens

For every man shall bear his own burden.
— GALATIANS 6:5

1. The scripture for this vignette admonishes every man to "bear his own burden." List five of the added responsibilities that the president is expected to carry out today that you think could be successfully taken on by others, such as state governments.

2. Circle the correct answer: The federal government is better able than the states to take care of most of the needs of the people.
   True   False

3. In your opinion, does a person function better when he has a few important responsibilities, or when he has a dozen responsibilities? Explain your answer below.

_____
_____
_____
_____
_____
_____
_____
_____

10.2 | Serving as President
Leading with Integrity

He that walketh uprightly walketh surely: but he that perverteth his ways shall be known.

— Proverbs 10:9

1. When taking the oath of office, the president promises to do two things. Write both of those promises below.

_____
_____
_____
_____

2. What is the definition of integrity? If you do not know, look it up or ask an adult. Write the definition below.

_____
_____

3. Explain in three sentences why it is important for the president to have integrity.

_____
_____
_____
_____
_____
_____
_____
_____
_____
_____

10.3 | Electing the President: The Electoral College
Wise Discernment

Finally, brethren, whatsoever things are true . . . honest . . . just . . . pure . . . lovely . . . of good report; if there be any virtue, and if there be any praise, think on these things.
— Philippians 4:8

1. As the Constitution was originally written, the president was elected by individuals carefully selected by each state, not directly by the people themselves. Explain why the Founding Fathers did not think the president ought to be elected by popular vote of the people.

_____
_____
_____
_____

2. Fill in the blank with the correct answer: "To avoid manipulation, corruption, and outside influences, electors were chosen for_____term(s)."

3. Imagine that you have been chosen as an elector and must select two people to nominate for president of the United States. Write a journal entry at least one paragraph long, explaining at least three characteristics you are looking for in a good president.

_____
_____
_____
_____
_____
_____
_____
_____

10.4 | The Supreme Court of the Land
Setting Boundaries

> *After the wisdom of thy God . . . set magistrates and judges, which may judge all the people . . . such as know the laws of thy God; and teach ye them that know them not.*
> — Ezra 7:25

1. There is currently no means by which a Supreme Court decision can be appealed or overturned. Why is this a problem? Explain in at least two sentences.

_____
_____
_____
_____
_____

2. Why is it appropriate for Congress to legislate (create and pass laws) but inappropriate for the Supreme Court to legislate? Write your answer below.

_____
_____
_____
_____

3. In at least one complete sentence, describe one limitation (listed in this vignette) that could be placed to limit the Supreme Court's unconstitutional decisions.

_____
_____
_____
_____

10.5 | The Workings of the Courts: State and Federal
Accepting Responsibility

And they judged the people at all seasons: the hard causes they brought unto Moses, but every small matter they judged themselves.

— Exodus 18:26

1. Circle the correct answer to fill in the blank: "State courts run according to their_____ (national, state) constitution."

2. What aspect of the British court system did the Founding Fathers implement in the Constitution? Answer below in at least one complete sentence.

_____
_____
_____
_____

3. The United States court system is designed for matters to be handled in the lower courts first, and then move to higher courts if necessary. Describe in two sentences why this is best for all concerned.

_____
_____
_____
_____
_____
_____
_____

10.6 | Trial by Jury
Compassion in Judgment

> *Judge not according to the appearance, but judge righteous judgment.*
> — JOHN 7:24

1. Choose all of the correct answer(s) that apply: Which of the following does a jury of peers not have power to do in today's courts?

    a) Pass an innocent or guilty verdict for a citizen on trial
    b) Judge the fairness of the law in a particular situation
    c) Decide what the law means

2. Explain in one or two sentences why the Founding Fathers originally gave juries the right to interpret and, in some cases, dismiss the law.

_____
_____
_____
_____
_____
_____

3. Read the scripture that accompanies this vignette. What do you think God means by "righteous judgment"? Explain in two or more sentences.

_____
_____
_____
_____
_____
_____

10.7 | Unity of the States
Working in Harmony

Let us therefore follow after the things which make for peace, and things wherewith one may edify another.
— ROMANS 14:19

1. Explain, in at least two sentences, one example mentioned in this vignette that requires states to work together.

_____
_____
_____
_____
_____
_____

2. Circle the correct answer: In order for all people to be treated equally and fairly, each state has to run its programs and manage its people the exact same way.   True   False

3. The name of our country is the United States of America. The states are united in many ways. Describe in one paragraph how these are truly the "United States."

_____
_____
_____
_____
_____
_____
_____
_____
_____
_____
_____

10.8 | Amending the Constitution
Guidance in Times of Change

> *I will instruct thee and teach thee in the way which thou shalt go: I will guide thee with mine eye.*
> — Psalm 32:8

1. What does it mean to amend something? If you don't know, look it up or ask an adult. Write the definition below.

_____
_____

2. Change can be good—but what happens if there is too much change? Describe what your life would be like if you moved to a new house every month, or if you got new parents every year, or if the days of the week changed around frequently. Choose one of these situations and explain in one paragraph the negative effects of this change.

_____
_____
_____
_____
_____
_____

3. When you need change, who are the most important people you can ask for advice to help you? Write them down, and explain your choices.

_____
_____
_____
_____
_____
_____

10.9 | Debts, Law, and Religion
Honorable Intentions

> *He shall be a vessel unto honour, sanctified, and meet for the master's use, and prepared unto every good work.*
> — 2 Timothy 2:21

1. During the time of the birth of the United States, it was common practice for many European nations to reject debts and not pay their creditors. Explain how the Founding Fathers prevented this dishonor from affecting the country after the Revolutionary War.

_____
_____
_____
_____

2. Choose the best answer: When government officials, such as the president of the United States, take the oath of office, they declare their honorable intentions to:

    a) uphold the Constitution.
    b) support the Constitution.
    c) defend the Constitution.
    d) all of the above
    e) none of the above

3. Imagine that you are working with a team of people to complete an assignment. One person differs from the rest and does not wish to cooperate. In your opinion, which is more important: satisfying the needs of one person, or accomplishing the group assignment? Explain your answer in at least three sentences.

_____
_____
_____
_____
_____

10.10 | Ratification and Authorization
Facing Uncertainty

Cast not away therefore your confidence, which hath great recompence of reward.
— Hebrews 10:35

1. What feeling do you think is the opposite of "uncertainty"? Write it below, and then explain the meaning of the word you chose.

_____
_____
_____

2. In your opinion, does someone feel uncertain only when he isn't sure he's right? Or can he feel uncertain or anxious about something even when he is sure he's right? Write your answer below.

_____
_____
_____
_____

3. Imagine that you are one of the signers of the Constitution. Write a one-paragraph journal entry dated the evening of September 17, 1787, after the signing of the Constitution. Write your feelings—do you have doubts about the future of your country? What are your hopes for its future?

_____
_____
_____
_____
_____
_____
_____
_____

Section Eleven

THE BILL OF RIGHTS AND THE AMENDMENTS

Introduction Activity

Section 11 details the twenty-seven Amendments added to the Constitution. First, complete all of Section 11. Then, in the space below, draw a poster that embodies, symbolizes, or explains one of the Amendments discussed in this section.

11.1 | First Amendment: The Right to Worship
Respect for All Worship

For all people will walk every one in the name of his god, and we will walk in the name of the Lord our God for ever and ever.
— MICAH 4:5

1. Choose the correct answer to fill in the blank: "The Constitution prohibits_____from sponsoring a specific religious denomination."

   a) the federal government
   b) the states
   c) both the federal government and the states
   d) neither the federal government nor the states

2. Why do you think the Founding Fathers specifically protected the freedom to worship in the first amendment that was added to the Constitution? Explain in at least two complete sentences.

_____
_____
_____
_____
_____

3. Choose the best answer: When voting on important decisions during election time, citizens are allowed to vote according to their beliefs and worship.   True   False

11.2 | First Amendment: The Right to Express Opinions
Respect the Opinions of Others

> *Who art thou that judgest . . . One man esteemeth one day above another: another esteemeth every day alike. Let every man be fully persuaded in his own mind.*
> — ROMANS 14:4–5

1. Using complete sentences, write one thing that could happen if the opinions of the people are disrespected or ignored.

_____
_____
_____
_____
_____

2. Make a list of at least three things a United States citizen can do to make his opinions known to the local or national government.

3. Imagine that someone you know wrote a newspaper article expressing an opinion you don't agree with. Describe in at least three sentences what your attitude and actions should be.

_____
_____
_____
_____
_____
_____
_____

11.3 | Second Amendment: The Right to Protect Ourselves
Protecting Ourselves and Others

If any provide not for his own, and specially for those of his own house, he hath denied the faith, and is worse than an infidel.

— 1 Timothy 5:8

1. Circle the correct answer to fill in the blank: "The Constitution allows _____ (the military, all citizens) the right to bear arms."

2. George Mason, one of our Founding Fathers, said that the best way for any government to enslave its people is to disarm them. Why does he compare disarmament to enslavement?

_____
_____
_____
_____
_____

3. In three sentences, share your opinion on how you think God feels about us protecting our families and ourselves.

_____
_____
_____
_____
_____
_____
_____
_____
_____

11.4 | Third and Fourth Amendments: The Right to Privacy
Safety and Refuge

Be still, and know that I am God... The Lord of hosts is with us; the God of Jacob is our refuge.

— PSALM 46:10–11

1. Think of a place where you feel safe and protected. Describe this place, and why you feel safe there. Use as many descriptive words as possible.

_____
_____
_____
_____
_____
_____

2. How is the right to keep our personal lives private a form of safety? Give at least one example to show how privacy can provide safety.

_____
_____
_____

3. The author tells us that there are some people who "believe that we have no need for privacy if we are doing nothing wrong." Do you believe this is true? Explain why or why not in one paragraph.

_____
_____
_____
_____
_____
_____
_____

11.5 | Fifth Through Eighth Amendments: The Rights of the Accused
The Lord's Law of Witnesses

One witness shall not rise up against a man for any iniquity ... at the mouth of two witnesses, or at the mouth of three witnesses, shall the matter be established.

— DEUTERONOMY 19:15

1. Circle the correct answer: People who are accused of crimes should not have any rights because they violated the law.   True   False

2. Why is it essential to have more than one witness testify for or against a person accused of a crime? Explain in two or more sentences.

_____
_____
_____
_____
_____
_____
_____

3. What is your responsibility as a United States citizen (and a moral person) if you see a crime committed or know of the guilt or innocence of another person? Respond in two sentences below.

_____
_____
_____
_____
_____
_____
_____
_____
_____

11.6 | Ninth and Tenth Amendments: Did We Forget Anything?
Usurping Rights

> *But whoso looketh into the perfect law of liberty, and continueth therein, he being not a forgetful hearer, but a doer of the work, this man shall be blessed in his deed.*
>
> —JAMES 1:25

1. What does the word "usurp" mean? If you don't know, look it up or ask an adult. Write the definition below. Then write one example of how a person's rights can be usurped by another person.

_____

_____

_____

_____

2. Circle all the answers that apply: The Tenth Amendment says that if any rights or freedoms are undefined or unmentioned, those rights and freedoms belong to whom?

   a) The federal government
   b) The military
   c) The states
   d) The people

3. United States citizens have the ability to prevent power-hungry individuals from usurping our rights. Three ways to do so include voting on Election Day, expressing your opinions to your local representatives, and staying informed. Writing one sentence per action, describe how each of these three actions can prevent our rights from being usurped.

_____

_____

_____

_____

_____

11.7 | Amendments Eleven, Twelve, Twenty, Twenty-Two, Twenty-Five, and Twenty-Seven: Polishing Procedures
Appropriate Place and Time

To every thing there is a season, and a time to every purpose under the heaven....

— Ecclesiastes 3:1

1. Circle the correct answer: The Founding Fathers knew the Constitution was not perfect and would eventually need changes.   True   False

2. Why might it be dangerous to America's freedoms for a president to serve in office for several terms? Write two reasons in the space below explaining how it is dangerous.

_____
_____
_____
_____
_____

3. The Founding Fathers included a process by which changes, or amendments, to the Constitution could be made. When something in a person's life needs to change, there is a process that God has made for him to do so. Fill in the missing letters in the word below to find out how people can change.

R _ P E N _ A _ _ E

11.8 | Amendments Thirteen, Fourteen, and Fifteen: The Right to Be Free
"Dwell Together in Unity"

Behold, how good and how pleasant it is for brethren to dwell together in unity!
— Psalm 133:1

1. There were good reasons why the Founding Fathers could not free all slaves in the Constitution. In one paragraph, write one of those reasons below, and explain how you feel about this reason.

_____
_____
_____
_____
_____
_____

2. What does the word "vindictive" mean? If you don't know, look it up or ask an adult. Write the definition below.

_____
_____
_____
_____

3. It is harder to achieve goals when people fight instead of working together. Think of a person you have difficulty living with in unity; then in the space below, write two things you can do to get along better, or unite, with that person.

_____
_____
_____
_____
_____

11.9 | Amendments Fifteen, Nineteen, Twenty-Three, Twenty-Four, and Twenty-Six: The Right to Vote
Everyone Has a Voice

For the body is not one member, but many.

— 1 CORINTHIANS 12:14

1. Circle the correct answer to fill the blanks for the following sentence from vignette 11.9 of the text:

"A _____ (democracy/republic) demands the unhampered _____ (vote/voice) of the people, and good government jealously protects the right to vote."

2. Look up the terms "democracy" and "republic," and write their definitions below. Then circle the term that describes America's government the way the Founding Fathers intended in writing the Constitution.

_____
_____
_____
_____

3. What do you think is the best age for voting—eighteen, twenty-one, or some other age? Give reasons for your position in your answer below, writing one paragraph.

_____
_____
_____
_____
_____

11.10 Amendments Sixteen, Seventeen, Eighteen, and Twenty-One: Unwise Transfer of Power
Using Our Agency

For it is God which worketh in you both to will and to do of his good pleasure.
— Philippians 2:13

1. The scripture for this vignette states that "it is God which worketh in" a person to help him choose to do what is right. Write one thing you can do to allow God to "work" within you.

_____
_____
_____
_____

2. Should government compel—or force—a person to do what is right? Explain why or why not below in one paragraph.

_____
_____
_____
_____
_____

3. Circle the correct answers to complete the sentence below:

"The Seventeenth Amendment doubled input from the _____ (states/people) and eliminated the _____ (states/people) in policymaking."

Section Twelve

WHO IS CHANGING THE CONSTITUTION?

Introduction Activity

In Section 7, you completed a word search. For Section 12, you will design the word search. As you read Section 12, select 15 words to include in your word search and enter them below—horizontally, vertically, forward, backward or diagonally. Select words that express important ideas, concepts, or people discussed in this section. List those words below the word search so that your audience knows what words to look for. Remember to fill in the leftover boxes with random letters. Once you have finished, ask a parent, teacher, or friend to complete your word search.

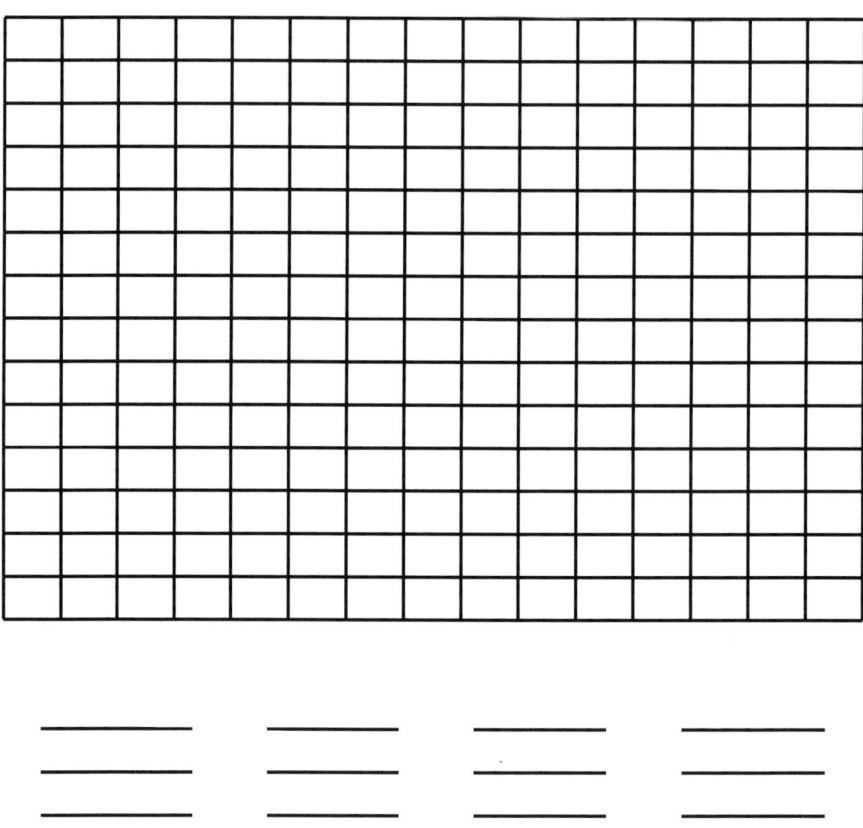

12.1 | Godless Philosophies: God versus Lucifer
Counterfeit Religion

> *The devil taketh him up into an exceeding high mountain, and sheweth him all the kingdoms of the world, and the glory of them; And saith unto him, All these things will I give thee, if thou wilt fall down and worship me. Then saith Jesus unto him, Get thee hence, Satan: for it is written, Thou shalt worship the Lord thy God, and him only shalt thou serve.*
> — Matthew 4:8–10

1. In Lucifer's counterfeit religion, who is being worshipped? Write your answer in a complete sentence.

2. Make a list of some of the things, people, and ideas that Lucifer's counterfeit religion attacks. Be sure that your list includes at least five things.

3. In one paragraph, explain how Lucifer's teachings make him an enemy to liberty and freedom.

12.2 | Godless Philosophies: Secular Humanism
Philosophies of Men

> *Beware lest any man spoil you through philosophy and vain deceit, after the tradition of men, after the rudiments of the world, and not after Christ.*
>
> — COLOSSIANS 2:8

1. Choose the best answer: Secular humanism believes that:

    a) men must save themselves, since God cannot save them.
    b) the meaning of life comes from man, not God.
    c) praying to God doesn't matter, because God is powerless.
    d) all of the above
    e) none of the above

2. The author states that many Christians "unwittingly" accept some of secular humanism's teachings, although those teachings oppose Christian values. Look up or ask an adult what "unwittingly" means, and write the definition below.

_____
_____

3. "Philosophy" that comes from men refers to the beliefs of men that are not inspired by God. Identify one philosophy or tradition of men from this vignette, and explain why you think people believe that mistaken idea.

_____
_____
_____
_____
_____
_____
_____
_____
_____

12.3 | Godless Philosophies: Creating Dependence
Becoming Independent

I will walk at liberty: for I seek thy precepts.
— Psalm 119:45

1. Circle the correct answer: According to the author, religion is not taught in public school classrooms today.   True   False

2. An entitlement mentality refers to people who believe that they deserve things they do not have to earn. How would an entitlement mentality lead people to be dependent on others or on the government? Explain below in at least two sentences.

_____
_____
_____
_____
_____
_____

3. Identify at least one way to learn to be independent and responsible as you gain an education.

_____
_____
_____
_____
_____
_____
_____

12.4 | Godless Philosophies: Setting the Stage
Being Unafraid

For God hath not given us the spirit of fear; but of power, and of love, and of a sound mind.
— 2 Timothy 1:7

1. The scripture for this vignette tells us, "God hath not given us the spirit of fear." If fear doesn't come from God, where do you think it comes from?

_____
_____
_____

2. The author highlights four steps that have been taken to create a climate of fear and lack of confidence in our country. Write down one of those steps, and explain how you can resist being affected by this action.

_____
_____
_____
_____
_____
_____
_____
_____
_____

3. The author states that faith is the opposite of fear. If we are to overcome fear, what can we have faith in instead? List at least three things you can have faith and hope about.

12.5 | Godless Philosophies: Our Government Today
Learning Correct Principles

If any man ... consent not to wholesome words, even the words of our Lord Jesus Christ ... He is proud, knowing nothing, but ... envy, strife, railings, evil surmisings, Perverse disputings of men of corrupt minds, and destitute of the truth ... from such withdraw thyself.
— 1 Timothy 6:3–5

1. Socialism is a system of government in which property and goods are owned and controlled by the government. Anything the people earn becomes the property of the government, which distributes those goods as it sees fit. Democratic socialism is one form of socialism described in this vignette. Describe it below in two sentences.

_____

_____

_____

_____

2. Circle the correct answer: Being misguided means that someone is evil or bad.   True   False

3. Christian principles and values are the opposite of socialism because God teaches that men are to work hard and benefit from the work of their own hands. How have Christian principles and values improved your life? Describe at least one situation in which knowing good, correct principles has helped you.

_____

_____

_____

_____

_____

_____

12.6 | Misuse of Constitutional Amendments: A Wise Amendment
Restoring What Was Lost

> *For, lo, the days come, saith the Lord, that I will . . . cause them to return to the land that I gave to their fathers, and they shall possess it . . . For I will restore health unto thee, and I will heal thee of thy wounds.*
>
> —JEREMIAH 30:3, 17

1. Circle the correct answer: The purpose of the Liberty Amendment is to undo all of the amendments and restore the Constitution to its original form before any amendments were passed.   True   False

2. How could we benefit from doing away with the Sixteenth Amendment? Describe at least two ways that lost freedoms can be restored through this action.

_____
_____
_____
_____

3. Write a journal entry as though you were Willis E. Stone, relating your reasons for designing the Liberty Amendment. Your journal entry should be at least one paragraph.

_____
_____
_____
_____
_____
_____
_____
_____
_____
_____

12.7 | Supreme Court Decisions: Judicial Review
"Act with Integrity"

> *The just man walketh in his integrity.*
> — Proverbs 20:7

1. The Constitution did not set judicial review as a responsibility of the Supreme Court. This procedure evolved during the first two decades under the Constitution. Summarize, in one sentence, the purpose of judicial review in the Supreme Court.

_____
_____
_____

2. Do you think that it is wise for Supreme Court justices to use their opinions, and not the Constitution, in making decisions? Explain why or why not in at least two sentences.

_____
_____
_____
_____
_____

3. Explain in one paragraph why it is equally important for everyday citizens like us to act with integrity.

_____
_____
_____
_____
_____
_____
_____
_____

12.8 Supreme Court Decisions: A Fixed Standard
Honoring Contracts

> *Brethren, I speak after the manner of men; Though it be but a man's covenant, yet if it be confirmed, no man disannulleth, or addeth thereto.*
>
> — GALATIANS 3:15

1. How would you define the noun "contract"? After looking up the definition, if needed, write it below.

_____
_____

2. How do the actions of the Supreme Court in not following the Constitution resemble changing the terms of a contract? Explain below.

_____
_____
_____
_____

3. Imagine the following scenario: You and a friend agree that you will pay him one dollar each time you borrow a movie from him. Then, after you borrow one of his movies, your friend tells you that you owe him five dollars because he is now charging five dollars each time you borrow a movie. How would you feel? What would you do? Write your answers below as though you were telling your friend what you think of this situation.

_____
_____
_____
_____
_____
_____

12.9 | Supreme Court Decisions: Unconstitutional Changes
Interpreting with God's Help

Now we have received, not the spirit of the world, but the spirit which is of God; that we might know the things that are freely given to us of God . . . which the Holy Ghost teacheth.
— 1 Corinthians 2:12–13

1. Finish this sentence: "It is especially important for Supreme Court justices to interpret the Constitution fairly because_____."

2. Each person has the ability to study a matter and make decisions. Why do you think it is important for us to have the right to make most decisions for ourselves, rather than having someone else make them for us? Explain below.

_____
_____
_____
_____
_____

3. Natural laws refer to consequences that automatically follow an action. For example, it is a natural law that if you throw a ball into the air, it will inevitably come back down. Natural laws can apply to morals and virtue as well. Write down two examples of natural laws that have to do with good and bad choices.

_____
_____
_____
_____
_____
_____
_____

12.10 Decline in Public Virtue: American Morality
"A Virtuous People"

> *As God liveth . . . while my breath is in me . . . my lips shall not speak wickedness, nor my tongue utter deceit . . . Till I die I will not remove mine integrity from me.*
>
> —Job 27:2—5

1. Examine the kinds of moral decay mentioned by the author in this vignette. Pick two that you have noticed and been concerned about. Then write a letter at least one paragraph long to a friend about those two examples of moral decay and why you are concerned.

___

2. The author states that people who are not virtuous are in need of greater rules and masters. Why do you think this is so? Explain below.

___

3. What can we do to emulate (follow) Job's example of standing true despite his sorrows and troubles? Use your own words to describe Job's feelings about integrity (found in the scripture for this vignette), and write them below.

___

12.11 | Decline in Public Virtue: Religious Worship
Anchoring Ourselves to Truth

> *Study . . . to work with your own hands.*
> — 1 Thessalonians 4:11

1. What is the purpose of an anchor? How does it help the ship? Write your answers below. Then describe what it means to "anchor" oneself to truth.

_____
_____
_____
_____
_____

2. Circle the best answer to fill in the blank: "Moral virtue can once again be restored to America, starting with_____."

   a) national government
   b) parents
   c) ourselves
   d) the media

3. George Washington said that two "indispensable supports" to political prosperity are religion and morality. What is an "indispensable support"? Look it up or ask an adult, and then write the definition. Describe what religion and morality have to do with political prosperity. Your answer should be at least one paragraph.

_____
_____
_____
_____
_____
_____
_____

12.12 | Decline in Public Virtue: Morality in Government
Selecting Moral Leaders

> *When the righteous are in authority, the people rejoice: but when the wicked beareth rule, the people mourn.*
> — PROVERBS 29:2

1. What can the people do when they are dissatisfied with their elected representatives? Write your answer below.

_____
_____
_____
_____

2. Create an acrostic for the words "moral leader" (read the workbook page for vignette 1.4, question one, for instructions on how to create an acrostic). Remember to use words, phrases, or sentences that describe what moral leaders are, or what moral leaders can do for their country.

3. There are several ways to ensure that only moral people serve in positions of leadership. Evaluate the ideas listed below and write "Yes" for each suggestion that will bring moral people to positions of leadership, and "No" for the suggestions that will not.

___ Be moral yourself
___ Only elect people who are in your political party
___ Ignore your elected representatives
___ Study the candidates
___ Vote for whomever your favorite actor says to vote for
___ Understand the problems

12.13 | Decline in Public Virtue: Entitlement Mentality
Learn to Love Work

In the sweat of thy face shalt thou eat bread, till thou return unto the ground.

— GENESIS 3:19

1. Choose the best answer(s) to fill in the blank: "The Declaration of Independence and Constitution promise that all Americans will have equal _____."

   a) money
   b) things
   c) beliefs
   d) freedoms
   e) justice

2. In the scripture for this vignette, Adam and Eve are told that they will have to provide for their own needs, such as food, "by the sweat of thy face." Based on this scripture, how hard should we be willing to work in order to provide for our families and ourselves? Explain your answer.

_____
_____
_____
_____
_____
_____

3. What does attitude have to do with learning to love work? Explain in at least one paragraph.

_____
_____
_____
_____
_____
_____

12.14 | Decline in Public Virtue: Moral Welfare
"Hard-Headed but Warm-Hearted"

Neither did we eat any man's bread for nought; but wrought with labour and travail night and day, that we might not be chargeable to any of you.

— 2 Thessalonians 3:8

1. Anyone receiving charity in American colonial times was expected to work for it. Do you think that asking a needy person to work for the help he is given is a form of compassion? Explain your answer below in at least two sentences.

_____
_____
_____
_____

2. What do you think it means to be "hard-headed"? Is this good or bad? Explain below in at least two sentences.

_____
_____
_____
_____

3. The colonists practiced what the author calls "wise compassion." Write down one example of giving without expecting anything in return and one example of giving while wisely expecting action from the person receiving help. Your examples can come from personal experience or from what you've observed.

_____
_____
_____
_____
_____

12.15 | Decline in Public Virtue: Distraction
Effects of the Media

By much slothfulness the building decayeth; and through idleness of the hands the house droppeth through.
— ECCLESIASTES 10:18

1. Circle the correct answer: Leisure and entertainment should be eliminated from our lives because they can be distracting and cause laziness.
    True   False

2. List three forms of idle or unwise use of entertainment. Next to each, write one possible negative consequence that comes from participating in that kind of entertainment.

3. Create two lists: one list of appropriate, healthful forms of entertainment; and one of enjoyable ways to spend your time that do not involve what we typically consider "entertainment" (things like finding shapes in the clouds, talking with family members, and so forth). Include at least three things on each list.

12.16 Decline in Public Virtue: Apathy—and Hope
Hope in Action

> *Wherefore gird up the loins of your mind, be sober, and hope to the end for the grace that is to be brought unto you.*
> — 1 Peter 1:13

1. What is apathy? Look up the definition or ask an adult, then write it below. Then write one word that would be the opposite, or antonym, of apathy.

_____
_____
_____

2. What happens in a group when the majority is apathetic? What happens in a group when the majority is actively involved? Which group would you prefer to be a part of? Write one sentence to answer each question (three sentences total).

_____
_____
_____
_____
_____
_____
_____

3. Choose the best answer: When a problem occurs, what is the best thing to do?

    a) Wait for a miracle.
    b) Hope that someone will help you.
    c) Do something without giving it much thought.
    d) Think about the problem, then act to create a solution.
    e) none of the above

Section Thirteen

FOUR ACTIONS TO REGAIN OUR ORIGINAL FREEDOMS

Introduction Activity

Section 13 outlines specific things we can do to regain America's freedoms, as a people and as a country. First, complete Section 13. Then, in the blank comic strip below, illustrate a scenario that shows how someone can do one of the four things (described in Section 13) to regain our freedoms. Be sure to use dialogue or narration in your comic strip.

13.1 | Simple Truths in the Constitution
God Works through Simple Things

God hath chosen the foolish things of the world to confound the wise; and God hath chosen the weak things of the world to confound the things which are mighty; And base things of the world, and things which are despised . . . to bring to nought things that are.
— 1 Corinthians 1:27–28

1. Circle the correct answer: God expects us to perform large-scale miracles and expensive projects in order to make a difference in the world.
True   False

2. The following sentence is taken from the vignette: "Those who read the Constitution *in the dialect of the Holy Spirit* will learn that God testifies of its truth." In one or two sentences, explain what you think the italicized part of the sentence means.

_____
_____
_____
_____
_____
_____
_____

3. The author writes, "We are asked to do the simple things that bring about peace. These things are to be done within our homes and communities." What simple things can you and your family do, in your home, to bring about peace? Make a list of at least three things.

13.2 | Look to God for Freedom
Turn to God

How often would I have gathered thy children together, even as a hen gathereth her chickens under her wings, and ye would not!

— MATTHEW 23:37

1. The expressions "turn to God" and "look to God" don't actually mean that you turn your head or look with your eyes. The actions of "turning" and "looking" to God are symbolic of spiritual actions. What do you think the words "turn" and "look" mean, as used in this vignette? Explain in one or two sentences.

_____
_____
_____
_____
_____

2. How is God the source of our freedoms when history tells us that men wrote the Declaration of Independence and the Constitution? Explain below.

_____
_____
_____
_____

3. Why does God sometimes wait for us to ask for His help instead of helping us without being asked? Explain what you think below.

_____
_____
_____
_____
_____

13.3 | Quality Family Life: Prayer
The Power of Prayer

The Lord is nigh unto all them that call upon him, to all that call upon him in truth.

— Psalm 145:18

1. Choose the correct answer(s) to fill in the blank: "Praying together as a family can _____."

    a) bind parents and children together
    b) help a family solve its problems
    c) bring greater peace to the family
    d) bring protection to family members
    e) all of the above

2. Write down one thing that children can learn from their parents, grandparents, and other family members through praying together.

_____
_____
_____
_____
_____

3. Set a goal to pray for something or someone specific for the next three days. Write down your goal below.

_____
_____
_____
_____
_____
_____

13.4 | Quality Family Life: Family Time Together
Spending Time Together

> *For where two or three are gathered together in my name, there am I in the midst of them.*
>
> — MATTHEW 18:20

1. Circle the correct answer: Spending family time together benefits more people than just the family members.   True   False

2. Can family time be beneficial for all families, regardless of their religious beliefs? Write down at least two benefits that come from family time that can benefit all families.

_____
_____
_____
_____
_____
_____
_____
_____

3. Think of at least three activities that you would like to do with your family for family time. Select activities that everyone can participate in and write them below. Share your list with your family.

13.5 | Quality Family Life: Study God's Word
Spiritual Armor

Wherefore take unto you the whole armour of God, that ye may be able to withstand in the evil day, and having done all, to stand. Stand therefore, having your loins girt about with truth, and having on the breastplate of righteousness; And your feet shod with the preparation of the gospel of peace; Above all, taking the shield of faith, wherewith ye shall be able to quench all the fiery darts of the wicked. And take the helmet of salvation, and the sword of the Spirit, which is the word of God.
— Ephesians 6:13–17

1. Fill in the blank with the correct answer: "Parents of colonial America taught their children from mostly one textbook, which was_____."

2. How do you think reading and studying the scriptures function as armor for young people today? Explain your opinion below.

_____
_____
_____
_____

3. Briefly tell about your favorite story or character from the Bible and explain why it is your favorite.

_____
_____
_____
_____
_____
_____
_____
_____

13.6 | Quality Family Life: Faith, Hope, and Charity
Faith, Hope, and Charity in Action

Who knoweth whether thou art come to the kingdom for such a time as this?
— ESTHER 4:14

1. Mordecai's question, "Who knoweth whether thou art come to the kingdom for such a time as this?" was an expression of faith in God's plan for Esther and the Jews. Write one thing that you can do to strengthen your faith to the point that you will be ready and willing to accept God's call to action in your life.

_____
_____
_____
_____

2. Which of the following words does the author use to describe hope?
   a) Expectation
   b) Faith
   c) Demand
   d) none of the above

3. It is easy to show charity to people you love or care about. However, we are commanded to show charity, or love, toward everyone, even our enemies. In one or two sentences, describe at least one way in which you can show charity toward someone you either don't know or don't like.

_____
_____
_____
_____
_____
_____
_____

13.7 Study the Constitution, Teach It to Our Families
Generations of Patriots

Hear this, ye old men, and give ear, all ye inhabitants of the land. Hath this been in your days, or even in the days of your fathers? Tell ye your children of it, and let your children tell their children, and their children another generation.

—Joel 1:2–3

1. Choose the best answer to complete the following statement: Studying the Constitution is extremely important to American citizens today because we:

   a) need to teach our children about the Constitution.
   b) are supposed to supervise our elected officials.
   c) should know about the freedoms we have.
   d) all of the above

2. Circle the correct answer: People do not read the Constitution today because it is too hard to read.   True   False

3. Generations refer to past, present, and future individuals. Write a paragraph telling about patriots you admire and why. Include a patriot from the past and one from the present. Finish by explaining, in at least one sentence, one way in which we can prepare people today to become the patriots of tomorrow.

_____
_____
_____
_____
_____
_____
_____
_____
_____
_____
_____

13.8 Get Involved: Local Efforts, National Effects
Joining Forces for Good

> *Fight the good fight of faith, lay hold on eternal life, whereunto thou art also called, and hast professed a good profession before many witnesses.*
>
> — 1 Timothy 6:12

1. The author writes, "As we receive training in the governing process, we can accept responsibilities at higher government levels if we choose." How does a person "receive training" in the way government runs?

___

2. Is it possible for just one person to make a difference? How? Explain your answer below.

___

3. Make a list of three things that a person your age could do to get involved in a good cause for our country. These can be small- or large-scale projects.

Section Fourteen

THE VISION FOR AMERICA

Introduction Activity

This final section shares the author's hope for the future of America. First, complete Section 14. Then, in the space below, write one paragraph describing what you think our country would be like if the changes detailed in Section 14 were to take place. Be as specific and detailed as possible.

After writing your paragraph, ponder it a while. Do you think the future you described is possible? Can you see America's future in sight? What are things you can do today to make your vision for America's future, OUR future, YOUR future, come true? Discuss these questions with a teacher, parent, or friend, or write your answers in a second paragraph below.

14.1 | Economics
Stability

God shall supply all your need according to his riches in glory by Christ Jesus.
— PHILIPPIANS 4:19

1. Circle the correct answer: It is always important to plan financially for emergencies because, even in a stable economy, there will be natural ups and downs.   True   False

2. What would be the effects of greater employment and fewer individuals and families that struggle financially? Describe this scenario in at least two sentences.

_____
_____
_____
_____
_____
_____
_____

3. In the author's vision of our future economic prosperity, what will be the reason for the average family's usable income essentially doubling? Answer in at least one sentence.

_____
_____
_____
_____
_____

14.2 | Education
Cultivating Patriotism and Love of Country

> *Therefore shall ye lay up these my words in your heart and in your soul... And ye shall teach them your children, speaking of them when thou sittest in thine house, and when thou walkest by the way, when thou liest down, and when thou risest up.*
> — Deuteronomy 11:18–19

1. What will be the benefit of having education standards set at the state level instead of the federal level?

_____
_____
_____

2. One way for parents to become more involved in their children's education is to homeschool their children. What benefits might come with homeschooling? Write down at least two benefits.

_____
_____
_____

3. Describe in one paragraph how you think teaching virtue and morality in home and school classrooms will improve students' lives.

_____
_____
_____
_____
_____
_____

14.3 | Business
Honesty with Others

Lord, who shall abide in thy tabernacle? Who shall dwell in thy holy hill? He that walketh uprightly, and worketh righteousness, and speaketh the truth in his heart. He that backbiteth not with his tongue, nor doeth evil to his neighbour . . . but he honoureth them that fear the Lord . . . He that doeth these things shall never be moved.
— Psalm 15:1–5

1. Choose the best answer to fill in the blank: "Businesses and jobs will greatly improve when _____ is (are) restored to the marketplace."

   a) honor
   b) virtue
   c) constitutional freedoms
   d) all of the above
   e) none of the above

2. The scripture for this vignette describes the virtues that God's people should practice. Write one sentence describing what it means to "walk uprightly," one describing what it means to "work righteousness," and one describing what it means to "speak the truth in his heart."

_____
_____
_____
_____
_____

3. Will eliminating most of the government regulations placed on the market mean that all business problems will go away? Explain why or why not in one or two sentences.

_____
_____
_____
_____

14.4 | Agriculture
Enjoying the Fruits of Our Labor

> *For thou shalt eat the labour of thine hands: happy shalt thou be, and it shall be well with thee.*
> — Psalm 128:2

1. Fill in the blank: "Those who are best suited to make decisions about what to grow, how to transport crops, and how much money to charge for them are the _____."

2. Why will food prices drop when large "agribusinesses" are no longer the government "favorites"?

_____
_____
_____

3. Imagine that you are a farmer who has grown only one major crop for the past ten years due to government regulations. Write a journal entry describing your feelings when you learn that government policies have changed and that you can now decide what is best to grow on your land.

_____
_____
_____
_____
_____
_____
_____
_____
_____
_____
_____
_____
_____

14.5 | The Family
Virtue in Families

Lo, children are an heritage of the Lord: and the fruit of the womb is his reward. As arrows are in the hand of a mighty man; so are children of the youth. Happy is the man that hath his quiver full of them.

— Psalm 127:3–5

1. Circle the correct answers to fill in the blanks: "The virtue in our _____ _____ (families, government) will cause our _____ _____ (families, government) to be more virtuous and moral."

2. What do you think the scripture for this vignette means by "children are an heritage of the Lord"? Write two sentences explaining your answer.

_____
_____
_____
_____
_____

3. In your opinion, what are the three most important things that parents can teach their children? Explain below in one paragraph.

_____
_____
_____
_____
_____
_____
_____
_____
_____
_____
_____
_____

MEET EXCITING PEOPLE THROUGH THESE BOOKS & DVDS

M ANY EXCITING BOOKS and DVDs tell the stories of the Constitution's history. Some of them are listed below. Have fun and enjoy yourself while learning more about the amazing history of our nation!

Books for Children

Benchley, Nathaniel. *Sam the Minuteman.* New York: HarperCollins, 1969. An easy-to-read account of Sam and his father fighting as minutemen against the British in the Battle of Lexington. 64 pages. Ages 5–9.

Edmonds, Walter D. *The Matchlock Gun.* New York: Dodd, Mead & Company, 1941. In 1756, during the French and Indian War in upper New York state, ten-year-old Edward is determined to protect his home and family with the ancient, and much too heavy, Spanish gun that his father had given him before leaving home to fight the enemy. 50 pages. Ages 8–12.

Fritz, Jean. *Shh! We're Writing the Constitution.* New York: Putnam, 1987. Describes how the Constitution came to be written and ratified. Also includes the full text of the document produced by the Constitutional Convention of 1787. 64 pages. Ages 9 and up.

—. *The Cabin Faced West.* New York: Coward-McCann, 1958. Life as it really was in late eighteenth-century America is portrayed through the life of ten-year-old Ann, who overcomes loneliness and learns to appreciate the importance of her role in settling the wilderness of western Pennsylvania. 124 pages. Ages 9 and up.

Gregory, Christina. *The Winter of Red Snow: The Revolutionary Diary of Abigail Jane Stewart.* New York: Scholastic, 1996. Eleven-year-old Abigail presents a diary account of life in Valley Forge from December 1777 to July 1778 as General Washington prepares his troops to fight the British. 173 pages. Ages 9–12.

Griffin, Judith. *Phoebe the Spy.* New York: Scholastic, 1977. During the Revolution, Phoebe Fraunces has a chance to save the life of General George Washington while he has dinner at Mortier House in New York City. Originally titled *Phoebe and the General.* 47 pages. Ages 9 and up.

Haley, Gail. *Jack Jouett's Ride.* New York: Viking Press, 1973. Recaptures the incident during the American Revolution when Jack Jouett rode to warn Thomas Jefferson and others of the coming of Tarleton's raiders. 31 pages. Ages 5–9.

Holbrook, Stewart, and Ernest Richardson. *The Swamp Fox of the Revolution.* New York: Random House, 1959. A biography of the American general who organized a guerrilla band to fight the British in South Carolina during the Revolution. 180 pages. Ages 9–12.

Howard, Ellen. *The Crimson Cap.* New York: Holiday House, 2009. Based on a true story and set in 1687, Pierre Talon, a ten-year-old French boy, travels with the famous explorer La Salle to find the Mississippi River. This exciting story opens windows into the lives of Americans a hundred years before the Constitution was written. 177 pages. Ages 9–12.

Kirkpatrick, Katherine. *Redcoats and Petticoats.* New York: Holiday House, 1999. Members of a family in the village of Setauket on Long Island are displaced by the Redcoats and serve as spies for the Revolutionary Army of George Washington. 32 pages. Ages 5–9.

McGovern, Ann. *The Secret Soldier: The Story of Deborah Sampson.* New York: Four Winds Press, 1975. A brief biography of the eighteen-year-old woman who disguised herself as a man and joined the Continental Army during the Revolutionary War. 62 pages. Ages 5–9.

Peacock, Louise. *Crossing the Delaware.* New York: Atheneum Books for Young Readers, 1998. Examines the events leading up to the Battle of Trenton, the battle itself, and its aftermath, as told through historical excerpts. 40 pages. Ages 9 and up.

Walker, Sally M. *The 18 Penny Goose.* New York: HarperCollins, 1998. Eight-year-old Letty attempts to save her pet goose from marauding British soldiers in New Jersey during the Revolutionary War. 61 pages. Ages 5–9.

Books for Teens

Bowman, David. *What Would the Founding Fathers Think? A Young American's Guide to Understanding What Makes Our Nation Great & How We've Strayed.* Springville, Utah: Plain Sight Publishing, 2012. A cartoon book, this volume tells the principles of the Constitution and their alterations through dialogue between the Reader and three Founding Fathers. George Washington, Benjamin Franklin, and James Madison arrive in the present via a Franklin invention to see how the Constitution is faring in the modern world. 119 pages. Ages 12 and up.

Brady, Esther. *Toliver's Secret.* New York: Crown Publishers, 1976. During the Revolutionary War, a ten-year-old girl crosses enemy lines to deliver a loaf of bread containing a message for the patriots. 166 pages. Ages 12 and up.

Clapp, Patricia. *I'm Deborah Sampson: A Soldier in the War of the Revolution.* New York: Lothrop, Lee & Shepard, 1977. Relates the experiences of the woman who disguised herself as a man in order to enlist and fight in the American Revolutionary war. 176 pages. Ages 12 and up.

Durrant, Lynda. *Betsy Zane, the Rose of Fort Henry.* New York: Clarion Books, 2000. In 1781, twelve-year-old Elizabeth Zane leaves Philadelphia to return to her brothers' homestead near Fort Henry in what is now West Virginia, where she plays an important role in the final battle of the American Revolution. 198 pages. Ages 12 and up.

Forbes, Esther. *Johnny Tremain.* Boston: Houghton Mifflin, 1943. A skillful silversmith's apprentice in eighteenth-century Boston loses the use of his hand after some other apprentices play a practical joke. Despite this change in his life, Johnny joins in the fight against the British and becomes a rider for the *Boston Observer* and a messenger for the patriots who planned the Boston Tea Party. He gradually becomes less bitter, finding new strength and courage as he grows into a man. 346 pages. Ages 12 and up.

Harlow, Joan Hiatt. *Midnight Rider.* New York: Margaret K. McElderry Books, 2005. In Boston in 1775, orphaned fourteen-year-old Hannah is indentured to the family of a British general and begins attending secret meetings disguised as a boy. She then passes warnings to the revolutionaries using her beloved horse, Promise. 404 pages. Ages 12 and up.

Klass, Sheila. *Soldier's Secret.* New York: Henry Holt, 2009. During the Revolutionary War, a young woman named Deborah Sampson disguises herself as a man in order to serve in the Continental Army. 215 pages. Ages 12 and up.

Lenski, Lois. *Indian Captive: The Story of Mary Jemison.* New York: Frederick A. Stokes Co., 1941. Fifteen-year-old Mary Jemison was captured by Indians and carried from her family farm in Pennsylvania in 1758. Through the years she struggled to maintain her English heritage and came to be known as the White Woman of the Genesee. 320 pages. Ages 12 and up.

Peck, Robert Newton. *Hang for Treason.* Garden City, NY: Doubleday, 1976. A Vermont boy becomes involved with Ethan Allen and the Green Mountain Boys despite his father's Tory leanings in the early days of the war. 232 pages. Ages 12 and up.

Speare, Elizabeth George. *The Witch of Blackbird Pond.* Boston: Houghton Mifflin, 1958. Kit Tyler must leave her Caribbean home to join the stern Puritan community of her relatives in Connecticut. She feels caged, until she meets the old woman known as the Witch of Blackbird Pond. But when their friendship is discovered, Kit herself is accused of witchcraft. 249 pages. Ages 9 and up.

Wibberley, Leonard. *John Treegate's Musket.* New York: Ariel Books, 1959. Loyalty to the British king was important to John Treegate—even more important than his son. But following his son's return from sailing the ocean, the two join together to fight for the colonies. First in a series of four books. 188 pages. Ages 12 and up.

Media

Arbon, Val. *Which Way, America?* Digital video disc. Produced by Val Arbon. Provo, UT: James Madison Institute, 2012.

O'Donnell, Kevin, and Michael Maliani. *Liberty's Kids.* Digital video disc. Directed by Judy Reilly. Burbank, CA: DIC Entertainment; Los Angeles, CA: Shout! Factory, 2002.

Slover, Tim. *A More Perfect Union.* Digital video disc. Directed by Peter N. Johnson. Provo, UT: Brigham Young University, 1989. This motion picture was officially recognized by the Commission on the Bicentennial of the United States Constitution.